HEALTH REPORTS:
DISEASES AND DISORDERS

SKIN CANCER

CONNIE GOLDSMITH

TWENTY-FIRST CENTURY BOOKS
MINNEAPOLIS

I dedicate this book to my mother, Alice, who died from melanoma long before
we knew about the dangers of too much sun. Special thanks to my writing group,
Jeri Chase Ferris, Erin Dealey, Patricia M. Newman, and Linda Joy Singleton for
their valuable help.

Twenty-First Century Books
A division of Lerner Publishing Group, Inc.
241 First Avenue North
Minneapolis, MN 55401 U.S.A.

Website address: www.lernerbooks.com

Library of Congress Cataloging-in-Publication Data

Goldsmith, Connie, 1945–
    Skin cancer / by Connie Goldsmith.
        p.   cm. — (USA Today health reports: diseases and disorders)
    Includes bibliographical references and index.
    ISBN 978-0-7613-5469-7 (lib. bdg. : alk. paper)
    1. Skin—Cancer—Juvenile literature. I. Title.
  RC280.S5G65 2011
  616.99'477—dc22   2010010003

Manufactured in the United States of America
1 – DP – 7/15/10

CONTENTS

USA TODAY
HEALTH REPORTS:
DISEASES AND DISORDERS

THE BODY'S LARGEST ORGAN

The body's largest organ is not the heart or the brain. It's not the lungs or the liver. The body's largest organ is the skin that covers you from head to toe. A person's skin weighs about 9 or 10 pounds (4 to 4.5 kilograms). That's triple the weight of the body's second largest organ—the liver. If someone's skin were stretched out, it would cover 20 to 22 square feet (about 2 square meters).

An organ is a collection of cells and tissues that work together to perform certain functions. For example, skin keeps you warm and cools you off. It keeps you from drying out in the sun or getting waterlogged in the pool. Skin is soft and stretchy so you can jump and dance and run. Yet it's tough enough to protect your muscles and bones. It's strong enough to hold all your organs in place. Skin never fails like a heart or liver. It is a miracle fabric that never wears out.

Even though skin performs dozens of important jobs, it doesn't get the respect it deserves. Skin asks only one thing of us—to protect it from the sun. For despite skin's strength, the ultraviolet radiation found in sunlight can damage it. It only takes a couple of childhood sunburns to increase the risk for getting skin cancer later in life. Even without burning, years of exposure to the sun while working outside or playing outdoor sports increases a person's chance of getting skin cancer.

When the ultraviolet radiation in sunlight damages skin cells, they may grow into tumors. A tumor is a general name for a collection of abnormal cells. Using tanning beds can be just as dangerous as getting sunburned. There are three common forms of skin cancer. They are named for the type of skin cell where each begins: basal cell carcinoma, squamous cell carcinoma, and melanoma.

More than 1 million Americans are diagnosed with skin cancer each year. Each year 11,600 of them die from it. The number of

Spending time in the sun without sunscreen can bring on skin cancer later in life.

people with melanoma, the most dangerous kind of skin cancer, has steadily increased since 1970. Doctors blame most of the rise in skin cancer on the increased amount of time people are spending in the sun. In the United States, melanoma is the second most common cancer among adolescents and young adults between fifteen and twenty-nine years of age.

Yet skin cancer is largely preventable. When people protect themselves from the sun and use sunscreen, the risk of developing skin cancer drops sharply. And if detected early enough, most skin cancer can be treated and cured.

Meet Caryn, Anne, Alexandria, Jerry, Ginger, Nate, Brian, Jay, and MaryAnn. Skin cancer has touched all of their lives.

USA TODAY

Caryn has had dozens of precancerous lesions (spots on the skin that may turn into cancer) and two different types of skin cancers removed over the past few years. As a teenager, she swam, biked, and hiked without using sunscreen. That wasn't unusual. In those days, most people wanted dark tans. They didn't know how dangerous too much sun could be.

Anne noticed an unusual freckle on her knee. It was round and black, much different from her other freckles. Her doctor wasn't too worried because the spot didn't look like a typical melanoma. Fortunately, he performed a biopsy to be sure. The results showed that the "freckle" was a melanoma.

Alexandria is a high school student in Texas. It's hard for her to tan, so she often fails to use sunscreen. One day at the pool, she burned so badly that she had huge blisters on her skin. Sometime later, a doctor told Alexandria that the spots that appeared on her abdomen were the precancerous condition called actinic keratosis.

Jerry noticed an odd, red spot on his face when he was twenty-five. At first, he thought it was just a pimple. But instead of healing, it crusted over and bled. That was enough to send him to see a dermatologist, a doctor who specializes in skin conditions. The doctor told Jerry he had a type of skin cancer called basal cell carcinoma.

Ginger spent a lot of time going to the beach and camping in the desert when she was a kid. Back then, nobody knew much about the relationship between the sun and skin cancer. She's had many basal cell carcinomas and two large squamous cell carcinomas removed. Her doctor predicts she will get more.

Nate spent a lot of time in tanning salons when he was twenty-two. First, he burned, then peeled, and then tanned. One day he noticed a dime-sized black mark on his back. He ignored it for a year. Finally, he went to a doctor who performed a biopsy. It showed that Nate had melanoma and that it had spread to other parts of his body.

Brian is a teacher who worked as a lifeguard when he was in college. He found a melanoma on his face that had spread to his neck. After Brian recovered from treatment, he began to talk to high school students about melanoma. A senior named Jay heard Brian talk. Jay found a mole on his back that turned out to be cancer.

MaryAnn went to a tanning salon nearly every week to improve her looks. When she was twenty-four, she noticed an unusual pink blemish on her face. It was too dark to hide with makeup. A plastic surgeon removed the spot. The next day, he told MaryAnn that she had melanoma.

This book will tell you about skin—what it is and how it works. It will describe the different types of skin cancer and how to prevent them. You will learn how skin cancer is diagnosed and treated. And you will read about intriguing new research into the causes of skin cancer. Read on to learn more about skin, your body's largest organ.

CHAPTER ONE

THE SKIN

Caryn has been fighting skin cancer for more than twenty years. "In my thirties, I began to have rough spots on my face," she said. "The dermatologist used liquid nitrogen to freeze the spots. Sometimes, it was five or six spots per visit. My doctor called these precancerous lesions. In my forties, I noticed an area on my temple that itched and bled. I ignored it for a few months, hoping it was another precancerous lesion. When I finally saw my dermatologist about it, he examined it. It turned out to be squamous cell cancer. It had spread too far and was too deep for him to remove it. He sent me to a plastic surgeon, who had to cut out a big area of skin to get rid of all the cancer."

Most people don't think about their skin very often unless something goes wrong with it. We are born nearly hairless, wrapped in and protected by our skin. Our skin is not perfect, but it is unique among warm-blooded animals. We are not covered by thick hair or feathers or fur. Most of our skin is nearly hairless compared to our fellow primates. This puts skin in close contact with the outside world. It allows for continual interaction with the environment.

Evolution fine-tuned our bodies to the environment. Skin comes in a wide variety of shades, ranging from very dark to very light. People whose ancestors lived nearest the equator in hot climates such as Africa have the darkest skin. This offered protection from the sun where it was most needed. Those whose ancestors lived in cold climates such as northern Europe have the lightest skin. These people had less need for such protection.

Skin provides a natural surface for decoration. It's like a canvas that tells the world who we are or who we want to be. Cultures around the world pierce their skin or mark it with tattoos or scars.

Human skin tones range from very light to very dark. People whose ancestors lived in hot climates tend to have darker skin than those whose ancestors came from the far north.

Many people paint their skin with cosmetics to brighten their cheeks and lips or to highlight their eyes. Skin may reveal our inner feelings. We blush when embarrassed and turn pale when frightened. Skin often reflects our state of health—the gray of illness, the flush of fever, or the yellow tinge of liver disease. Skin hints at our age: the firm elastic skin of youth, the dry wrinkles of old age.

Every body system has a proper name. The heart is part of the cardiovascular system. The stomach and liver are part of the digestive system. The skin is sometimes called the integumentary system.

The skin is a complex organ made up of several layers that contain different types of cells. Skin also performs many specialized functions that help us to survive. Knowing about the kinds of cells and tissues in skin makes it easier to understand skin cancer.

MEET YOUR SKIN

Skin is very thin. On most parts of the body, it's about 0.04 to 0.08 inches thick (1.0 to 2.0 millimeters). The skin on the palms of the hands and the soles of the feet is a little thicker—nearly 0.25 inches (6.0 mm). Skin is made up of three even thinner layers known as the epidermis, the dermis, and the hypodermis. The hypodermis is also called the subcutis or the subcutaneous tissue.

EPIDERMIS

The epidermis is the outer layer of the skin, the part that we see and touch. Unlike most parts of the body, the epidermis has no blood vessels. Even though the epidermis is only thirty to fifty cells thick, it is formed of five layers. From the innermost layer (stratum) to the outermost, they are: the stratum basale, the stratum spinosum, the stratum granulosum, the stratum lucidum, and the stratum corneum.

The stratum basale is a very thin layer of cells that lies over the basement membrane. This membrane separates the lowest level of the epidermis from the upper level of the dermis. The stratum basale contains the cells—known as basal cells—that make new skin cells. The basal cells and the new skin cells they make are collectively called epithelial cells. These cells cover our bodies on the outside and line many of our organs on the inside.

The millions of new epithelial cells formed in the stratum basale are continually moving upward to replace older cells. This explains why our skin easily heals from minor scrapes and scratches without scarring. The new epithelial cells migrate upward through the spinosum, granulosum, lucidum, and the corneum layers. As the epithelial cells move into the spinosum and granulosum layers, they mature into the oblong-shaped cells called squamous cells. Squamous cells are the most common cells in the epidermis. The majority of skin cancers start in the basal and squamous cells.

It takes about seven weeks for living epithelial cells produced in the stratum basale to move upward through the epidermis to the stratum corneum, the outermost layer of skin. By the time the epithelial cells reach the stratum corneum, they are basically dead. Cells in the stratum corneum no longer have a nucleus (the control center of a cell that holds the cell's genetic material).

The dead cells are flat and held together by lipids. Lipids are fatty, waxy substances that help to waterproof the skin. Every day we shed many thousands of dead, dried-up skin cells from the stratum corneum. These flecks of skin constantly fall from our bodies like microscopic snowflakes, landing on the floor, in our clothing, and at the bottom of the shower.

Other cells and structures reside within the epidermis. These are called non-epithelial cells. They are very different from the cells that make up most of the epidermis.

- Melanocytes are located in the basal layer of the epidermis. They make up 5 to 10 percent of cells in that layer. Melanocytes produce the pigment melanin, which gives skin its color. People with little melanin are light-skinned. Those with more melanin have darker skin. All people have about the same number of melanocytes. The difference in the amount of melanin produced determines skin color. The reddish hemoglobin found in red blood cells and the yellowish pigment carotene also influence skin color. Melanin helps to protect skin against the ultraviolet radiation in sunlight. Excess melanin production makes people tan. It's a signal that the skin is working hard to protect itself from the sun's ultraviolet radiation. The dangerous skin cancer known as melanoma starts in melanocytes.

LAYERS OF THE SKIN

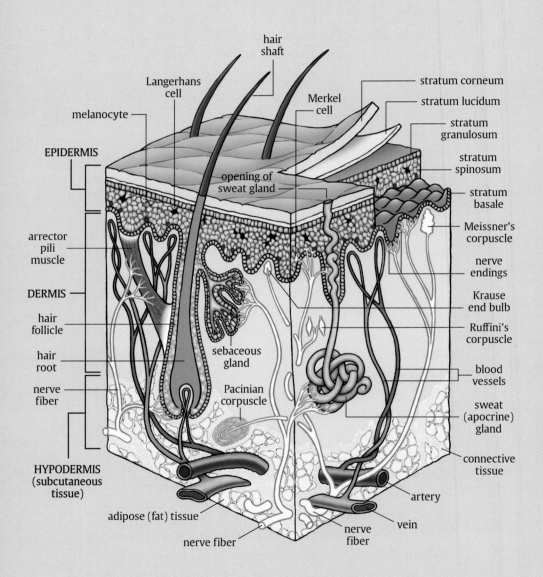

hair shaft

Langerhans cell

Merkel cell

melanocyte

EPIDERMIS

stratum corneum

stratum lucidum

stratum granulosum

stratum spinosum

opening of sweat gland

stratum basale

Meissner's corpuscle

arrector pili muscle

nerve endings

DERMIS

Krause end bulb

hair follicle

Ruffini's corpuscle

hair root

blood vessels

nerve fiber

sebaceous gland

sweat (apocrine) gland

Pacinian corpuscle

connective tissue

HYPODERMIS (subcutaneous tissue)

adipose (fat) tissue

artery

nerve fiber

vein

nerve fiber

- Langerhans cells are part of the body's immune system. These cells work to fight skin infections. When Langerhans cells come across invading pathogens (organisms that cause disease) such as bacteria, the cells capture the invaders and shunt them off to the nearest lymph node (small organs the size and shape of beans that are part of the immune system). Once in the lymph node, other parts of the immune system do their part to finish off the bacteria.
- Merkel cells are sensory cells found in the basal layer of the epidermis. They sense touch and hair movement. For example, the Merkel cells can feel a nearly weightless mosquito landing on your arm and moving a hair or two as it crawls over your skin. A very rare and dangerous skin cancer called Merkel cell carcinoma may form in these cells.

DERMIS

The dermis lies below the epidermis. The dermis is the thickest skin layer and helps to cushion and protect the body. Proteins called collagen and elastin in the dermis give skin its strength and flexibility. Blood vessels, nerves, glands, and other types of tissues make up the dermis. The following is a list of these and their functions:

- Sebaceous glands produce and secrete, or give off, sebum, the skin's natural oil.
- Apocrine glands produce and secrete sweat.
- Pacinian corpuscles sense deep pressure.
- Meissner's corpuscles sense light pressure.
- Krause end bulbs detect cold temperatures, as well as touch and pressure.
- Ruffini's corpuscles detect warm temperatures and skin stretching, as well as touch and pressure.

- Nerve endings detect pain.
- Hair roots and hair follicles originate in the dermis. The hair shaft reaches from the dermis through the epidermis and extends outside the skin.
- Arrector pili muscles control the movement of each hair. When people feel their "hair standing on end," these muscles are working.

HYPODERMIS

The hypodermis, or subcutaneous, tissue lies beneath the dermis. The hypodermis is composed of adipose tissue (fat), fatty lipids, connective tissue (tough, elasticlike fibers that help to hold cells and organs together), and blood vessels. The hypodermis holds the dermis to underlying muscle. It also cushions the body and regulates temperature. Women store more fat in the hypodermis than men. This extra subcutaneous fat gives women a soft body shape.

SKIN'S MANY JOBS

Some of the body's organs perform one specialized job. For example, the lungs exchange carbon dioxide for oxygen. The heart pumps freshly oxygenated blood to all parts of the body. Kidneys strain waste products from the blood and excrete them in urine. Eyes only see, and ears only hear. Other organs, such as the liver, perform many tasks. But the skin takes multitasking to a whole new level.

KEEPS US WARM

Skin helps to keep us warm in several ways. The fat stored in the hypodermis insulates us against the cold. The tiny hairs on our skin help trap heat and hold it close to the body. Shivering, which occurs all over the body, including the skin, radiates heat in an attempt to warm a very cold body. When a person is cold, blood vessels in the skin constrict and move deeper to conserve the heat in blood. This is why people look pale or even blue tinged when they are cold.

COOLS US OFF

The human body is designed to work best at a temperature of 98.6°F (37°C). Sweating, one of the most important bodily functions, plays a major role in keeping us from overheating. As air moves over sweat-slicked skin, the sweat evaporates. This evaporation helps to cool the body more quickly. The large surface of our skin allows more area for this evaporation to take place. Compare our sweating skin with how a dog sweats. Dogs sweat mostly through their tongues. When dogs are hot, they pant and their tongues hang out of their mouths. Moisture evaporates from the tongue to cool it off. But dogs' tongues have a very small surface area compared to the human skin. Dogs and many other animals cannot cool themselves as efficiently as people can.

People sweat a lot. Inactive people going about their usual activities sweat between 1 to 3.5 cups (300 to 800 milliliters) of fluid daily. A very active person who is exercising can sweat more than 5 quarts (5 liters) each day. People need to drink a lot of water to make up for that loss. When a person is overheated, blood vessels

During exercise or other times when bodies overheat, sweat glands in the dermis produce sweat. Sweat evaporates from the surface of the skin to cool the body.

April 20, 2009

From the Pages of USA TODAY

Where skin color matters
For black Americans, the sun is part of a revolving debate

Can dark skin be a health hazard? It might be—if you are a dark-skinned person who lives far from the equator, gets little sun exposure and consumes little vitamin D.

That describes many African Americans and helps explain why studies find that average African-American children and adults have much lower blood levels of the vitamin than white Americans do. Vitamin D is produced in response to sun exposure in a process that works most efficiently in pale skin. It's also in fortified dairy products and fatty fish, but few Americans consume enough of those foods to meet recommendations.

Just how much vitamin D Americans need and how they should get it is under debate. Scientists also are debating evidence that vitamin D, best known for building bones, can lower the risk of cancer, diabetes, heart disease and other ailments.

And they are asking this intriguing question: Could varying vitamin D levels contribute to the health gap between black and white Americans?

in the skin dilate and move upward to release excess heat from the blood. This is why peoples' faces turn red when they are very hot, for example, or when they have exercised vigorously or are sunburned.

MAKES VITAMIN D

Sunlight works with chemicals in the epidermis to make vitamin D. This important vitamin helps to maintain normal levels of calcium and phosphorus in the body. These minerals are essential for the formation of healthy bones and teeth. Researchers believe vitamin D may help prevent cancers of the prostate, the breast, the pancreas,

Boston University professor Michael Holick, a leading vitamin D researcher, says yes: "We think it's why African Americans develop more prostate cancer, breast cancer and colon cancer."

John Flack, principal investigator at the Center for Urban and African American Health at Wayne State University, Detroit, says: "I think it's potentially a very important explanation for some of the differences, from hypertension to cancer to heart failure. The actual proof is not there, but it's plausible."

Someone in Boston with pale skin can get adequate vitamin D by exposing their arms and legs to the sun for 10 to 15 minutes twice a week in the summer. Someone with the darkest skin might need two hours of exposure each time, Holick says.

Dermatologists also warn that sun exposure increases the risk of skin cancer and wrinkling, even in dark-skinned people.

How much is enough? Holick endorses "sensible, limited sun exposure" but says it's also time to recommend that everyone, regardless of skin color, take a daily vitamin D supplement of at least 1,000 international units (IU).

Not all scientists agree, but an expert panel at the non-profit Institute of Medicine is reviewing recommended daily intakes, now at 200 IU for people up to age 50, 400 IU for people ages 51 to 70 and 600 IU for those over age 70. An 8-ounce [0.2-liter] glass of fortified milk contains 100 IU.

"All Americans, but particularly people with darker skin, should pay attention" to new guidelines, says Adit Ginde, a researcher at the University of Colorado Denver School of Medicine. Ginde led a study, published in the Archives of Internal Medicine, that found that vitamin D levels are falling in all racial groups but are especially low in African Americans.

—Kim Painter

---

the ovaries, and the colon as well.

While too much sun can lead to skin cancer, too little can lead to vitamin D deficiency. It takes a light-skinned person without sunscreen just ten to fifteen minutes of sunshine a few days each week to make enough vitamin D. Darker-skinned people need more time in the sun to make the same amount of vitamin D. Other sources of vitamin D are dietary supplements (vitamin pills), foods such as oily fish (tuna, salmon, and mackerel), and eggs. Vitamin D is added to foods such as milk and other dairy products, orange juice, and some breakfast cereals.

www.usatoday.com

USA TODAY

Life

SECTION D

August 3, 2009

From the Pages of USA TODAY

Kids could suffer later for lack of vitamin D
Bone, heart risks increase

Seven out of 10 children and young adults don't get enough vitamin D, which could increase their risk for bone and heart problems, a study suggests.

A study of more than 6,000 children and young adults published in the journal *Pediatrics* had striking results, says lead author Michal Melamed, assistant professor of medicine and epidemiology at the Albert Einstein College of Medicine in New York.

"Seventy percent of children—millions of kids—have inadequate levels of vitamin D for bone health," Melamed says.

Researchers analyzed data on people ages 1 to 21 collected by the National Health and Nutrition Examination Survey. They discovered that 9% of the study sample—which projects to 7.6 million people age 21 and under in the USA—were vitamin-D-deficient. An additional 61%, the equivalent of 50.8 million nationwide, had insufficient D levels.

D-deficiency was more common in older children as well as female, African-American, Mexican-American and obese kids, and in those who drank milk less frequently than once a week, Melamed says. D-deficiency was also more common in kids who spent more than four hours a day watching TV, playing video games or using computers.

"The study has enormous public health implications and heightens the concern about the health status of children," says vitamin D researcher JoAnn Manson, Chief of Preventive Medicine at Brigham and Women's Hospital in Boston.

Low vitamin D levels at such a young age could predispose them to other diseases later in life linked to D deficiency, including diabetes, hypertension, heart disease and cancer, Manson says.

Melamed says today's culture of computers, TV and video games, less milk drinking, and increased use of sunscreens, which block UV-B rays—the kind that help the body convert a form of cholesterol in the skin into vitamin D—are likely culprits in waning vitamin D levels among youngsters.

—*Mary Brophy Marcus*

PROTECTS US FROM THE ENVIRONMENT

Skin provides a waterproof barrier so that we don't swell up like a sponge when we shower or dry out like a raisin when we sit in the sun. Skin helps to protect us from many harmful substances in the environment. Skin gets thicker in response to environmental challenges. For example, too much sun can thicken the skin. Skin also forms calluses on parts of the body exposed to friction to protect deeper skin layers. This happens on the feet when people wear shoes that don't fit correctly. It happens on the hands when someone uses a particular tool or instrument frequently.

Many potentially harmful chemicals, such as those found in air pollution, roll right off intact skin. Few substances stain it. For example, spill ketchup or a blueberry smoothie on your favorite shirt and it's ruined. Spill it on your skin, and it washes right off. The layers of skin also form a cushion against minor injuries. If someone pokes your arm with a finger, your skin is not damaged. However, a finger poke to the brain would certainly cause injury.

PROTECTS US FROM GERMS

Skin keeps pathogens, disease-causing microorganisms such as bacteria and viruses, from entering the body. The dry, dead layers of the epidermis form a dense barrier that is nearly impossible for pathogens to penetrate. Immune cells in the epidermis help to defend us against these pathogens. The constant shedding of the outermost skin cells also decreases the chance that pathogens can gain entry into our bodies. Skin is slightly acidic, which also helps to repel pathogens. Of course, bacteria can readily enter the body through a cut or scratch in the skin.

While skin protects us from bad germs, it is also home to hundreds of millions of bacteria. Some of these members of our very own personal zoo are harmless. Others are helpful. A few are potentially dangerous if they enter our bodies. Dr. Elizabeth Grice, who worked on a study to identify bacteria normally found on skin, said, "Skin is home to vibrant communities of microbial life which may significantly influence our health." That study found an average of forty-four species of bacteria living on arms and nineteen species living behind ears. Just as a driver must compete for space on a crowded freeway, invading pathogens must compete for space with the bacteria that normally live on our skin. The invaders usually lose.

REDUCES BLOOD LOSS

Everyone gets minor cuts and scrapes on their skin, which easily heal. A deeper cut may slice into the blood vessels located at the bottom of the dermis and at the top of the hypodermis. The skin helps to control excess bleeding from such injuries. The blood vessels constrict (get smaller), decreasing blood flow to the area. Proteins in the blood and skin help the blood to clot. Then scabs form on the skin's surface to prevent body fluids from leaking out. Scabs also protect the healing tissues beneath the injury.

SELECTIVELY ABSORBS

Certain medications are well-absorbed through the skin. Some medications are delivered in patches that stick to the skin and release the drug over a period of hours or days. Nicotine patches designed to help people quit smoking may be the best known. Other medications commonly delivered in patches include those for pain, ADHD (attention deficit/hyperactivity disorder), motion sickness, and birth control. Scientists are working to develop a way to deliver a diabetic's insulin through skin patches. This means that people with diabetes would not have to receive their insulin by needle injection.

ELIMINATES WASTE PRODUCTS

The skin excretes excess water and salt. While the kidneys excrete most of the body's waste products as urea and uric acid in urine, the skin also excretes small amounts of these substances.

SKIN: STRONG YET FRAGILE

Our skin is a highly specialized organ that constantly communicates and interacts with the environment. It helps to keep us safe by alerting us to extremes of heat and cold, pain and pressure. Skin can feel the tiniest insect crawling on your arm or the lightest breeze blowing across your face. It presents an effective barrier to potentially dangerous germs and hazardous chemicals. Yet as strong as skin is, it's also highly vulnerable to damage from the ultraviolet radiation found in sunlight. With more than one million people developing skin cancer every year, that's important to remember.

Since Caryn had the squamous cell cancer removed, she's had several more precancerous lesions on her face and two basal cell cancers on her nose removed. "I wasn't careful with sunscreen when I was young. We didn't know any better in those days. I swam, biked, and hiked outdoors a lot. Now, I visit my dermatologist every six months for a skin exam. I wear hats and try to avoid sun exposure between noon and 4:00 P.M. I've invented what I call nighttime gardening, where I pull weeds and clip shrubs in the early evening."

What advice does Caryn have for teens? "I'd love teens to avoid what I went through. Wear sunscreen, and lots of it. Cover up with long sleeves and a hat. Avoid midday sun if you can. Make sure to check your skin for anything unusual. If you find something that worries you, get to a dermatologist right away."

CHAPTER TWO

CANCER AND SKIN

*A*nne watched a small, nearly black spot on her knee for about a year. It was the size of a freckle, round, and it didn't grow or change at all. The only thing that bothered her was that the spot was darker than her other freckles. "I'd spent much of my life pursuing the perfect suntan, sailing, riding, and doing all things sun," Anne said. "So when I turned forty-five, I started having a dermatologist check my skin each year. When I pointed out the spot to my doctor, he said he wanted to do a biopsy to make sure it wasn't anything to worry about."

Human cancer has been around for thousands of years. Some ancient skeletons show signs of cancer. Marks from what were probably basal cell carcinomas have been found on the dried flesh of mummies. Egyptian healers described cancer and how to treat it in two sets of manuscripts written on papyrus about 1600 B.C. Called the Edwin Smith and George Ebers Papyri, these manuscripts provide evidence of early Egyptian medicine.

This ancient Egyptian papyrus contains a description of cancer and its treatment. It was written about 1600 B.C.

Hippocrates, sometimes called the father of medicine, lived in Greece between 460 and 370 B.C. He examined the bodies of people who had died of odd growths called tumors. He noticed some tumors reached out with leglike protrusions and seemed to claw their way into surrounding organs. Hippocrates described them as looking like crabs scuttling sideways along a beach. He called them *karkinos*, which is Greek for "crabs." The word *cancer* comes from this word.

It took centuries to discover the true cause of cancer. Hippocrates believed that too much black bile in the body caused the disease. Doctors in ancient Greece believed that black bile was one of four so-called humors (substances) in the body. The other humors were blood, phlegm, and yellow bile. The humors had to be in balance for good health.

In the 1600s, an Italian doctor named Gaspare Aselli discovered the lymphatic system. He described the tiny tubes that branched throughout the body as being similar to the arteries and veins that carried blood. The lymphatic tubes carry a colorless fluid called lymph. For about two hundred years, doctors believed that lymph caused cancer as it circulated through the body. Since then, we've learned that the lymphatic system is an important part of our immune system.

During the 1800s, many scientists thought that irritation or accidental injury could cause cancer. For two hundred years, cancer was blamed on parasites such as ticks, fleas, and worms. In 1926 Dr. Johannes Fibiger received the Nobel Prize in Medicine for discovering that roundworms cause stomach cancer. He was not correct. In modern times, scientists and doctors have learned that genetic mutations—damage to a cell's DNA—cause most kinds of cancer. This includes skin cancer.

HEALTHY CELLS

The cell is the basic structure of all living things. Bacteria are made up of only one cell. It takes an estimated fifty to one hundred trillion cells to make up large complex organisms such as adult humans. The human body contains more than two hundred types of cells. Cells group together to form organs, such as the liver, the heart, the brain, and the skin. Each type of cell is different. When viewed under a microscope, scientists can identify which cells come from which organs.

Cells grow and divide rapidly during the early years of a person's life. Tiny fingers become big fingers. Little brains grow to adult size. Small hearts get large enough to pump 5 to 6 quarts (4.7 to 5.7 liters) of blood throughout the body. This rapid growth and division of cells slows dramatically in adulthood when people reach their full size.

Yet we still need to be able to make new cells because our bodies face continual damage and injury. A teen breaks her wrist while skateboarding. New bone grows to fix the break. A man slices his finger while preparing steaks for a barbecue. New skin grows to heal the injury. A surgeon cuts into a child's abdomen to remove a bad appendix. The child's body forms new skin, muscle, and blood vessels to repair the damaged tissues. Only a small scar remains. Other times, cells just wear out and must be replaced.

Cellular renewal is a constant process that maintains organs in a healthy and functional state. The body regulates this process so that just the right number of new cells are made—not too few, not too many. Each cell has a built-in sensor system to detect damage or injury.

When a cell discovers damage, it first tries to repair itself. If the damage is too great, the cell orders itself to stop growing and to self-destruct. Chemical changes inside the cell cause it to shrink. Nearby healthy cells absorb the destroyed cellular material. This self-destruction of damaged or sick cells is called apoptosis, the deliberate suicide of an abnormal cell.

WHEN GOOD CELLS GO BAD

When apoptosis fails, the rapid growth of abnormal cells can turn into cancer. The American Cancer Society defines cancer as a group of diseases characterized by the uncontrolled growth and spread of abnormal cells. Instead of the abnormal cells dying off as they should, they continue to grow and become cancerous. These cancer cells can grow into or invade other cells and tissues. This process is called metastasis. Normal cells cannot do this.

For example, cells from a melanoma on an arm can enter blood vessels in the dermis and hypodermis and be carried to the brain. Once in the brain, the melanoma cancer cells can spread and form one or more new tumors. A cancer such as this is called metastatic melanoma, not brain cancer. Cancers are named for the place where they start. Breast cancer that spreads to the liver is called metastatic breast cancer, not liver cancer. Prostate cancer that spreads to the bones is called metastatic prostate cancer, not bone cancer.

The word *tumor* is a general term for a mass of abnormal cells. Not all tumors are cancer. Tumors can be benign or malignant. Benign

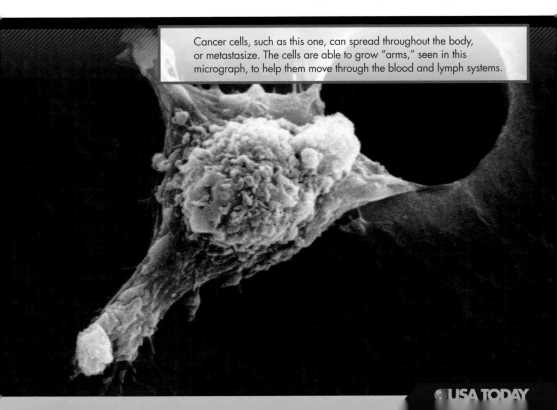

Cancer cells, such as this one, can spread throughout the body, or metastasize. The cells are able to grow "arms," seen in this micrograph, to help them move through the blood and lymph systems.

tumors do not invade adjoining tissues or spread to other parts of the body. However, depending on their size and where they are located, benign tumors can damage surrounding tissues and organs as they grow larger. For example, a meningioma is a benign brain tumor. It must be removed because it puts pressure on delicate parts of the brain as it grows. But meningiomas do not invade and destroy surrounding tissues. Benign tumors can be removed, and they do not usually grow back.

Malignant tumors are cancerous because cells in these tumors readily invade nearby tissues. Blood vessels can carry the cancerous cells to distant parts of the body where they form new tumors. Malignant tumors can be difficult to remove. And they may grow back unless every cancerous cell is located and cut out by a surgeon. Radiation and chemotherapy also help to kill cancer cells. Melanoma is a malignant skin cancer that can metastasize to distant parts of the body to form malignant tumors.

CAUSES OF CANCER

The most basic cause of cancer is genetic mutation. Genes are segments of DNA, the genetic blueprint that makes every organism what it is. Our DNA determines how tall or short we are, if we have brown eyes or blue, if we have black hair or blond. A mutation is a permanent change in the DNA of a cell. In some cases, the cell repairs the genetic mutation and the cell lives on normally. Sometimes the cell cannot be saved and apoptosis occurs. The damaged cell destroys itself.

Apoptosis doesn't always work the way it should. Sometimes the damaged cell survives and begins to divide. Each new cell contains the genetic mutation. As the mutated cells continue to divide, the initial mutation changes even more. These deformed mutated cells are aggressive and genetically unstable. The longer the mutated

National Cancer Registries

C ancer kills about fifteen hundred people each day in the United States. It has a devastating impact on patients and their families. In addition, cancer costs the nation well over $220 billion dollars per year in direct medical costs and lost productivity.

Hospitals and doctors around the nation report cancer statistics to state cancer registries. The states work with the Centers for Disease Control and Prevention to collect and analyze data about cancer cases and deaths. Reported cancers include melanoma; cancers of the breast, the lungs, the colon, and the prostate; and leukemia.

Cancer registries are designed to monitor cancer trends over time; determine cancer patterns in various populations (by age, gender, and state of residence); guide planning and evaluation of cancer programs; and to advance research.

Basal cell carcinomas and squamous cell carcinomas are not reported to cancer registries. Scientists can only estimate how many people develop those types of skin cancers.

cells continue their uncontrolled growth, the more abnormal and dangerous they are. They may grow into a cancerous tumor.

Genetic mutations cause cancer, but what causes genetic mutations? Genetic mutations can happen in several ways. For example, they may be inherited. Such inherited mutations substantially increase the risk that a person will develop a specific cancer. For example, there is a gene called *BRCA1*. Mutations in this gene may lead to breast cancer. Mutations in *BRCA1* often can be identified in families that have a higher than average number of people with breast cancer. Mutations in a gene known as *PATCHED1* may lead to basal cell carcinoma. Yet not every person with an inherited genetic mutation will develop cancer.

Some genetic mutations just happen, much like making a spelling error in your homework. When trillions of cells are growing and dividing and repairing themselves, it is not unusual for a genetic mutation to occur naturally. This is called a sporadic mutation. Cancers developing from such mutations are called sporadic cancer. Most of these forms of cancer develop from epithelial cells, the cells that make up the skin and line certain organs and tissues. Sporadic cancers include cancer of the intestines, ovaries, and the non-melanoma skin cancers—basal cell and squamous cell carcinoma.

Not every genetic mutation is harmful. Some may even give an organism a survival advantage. Many scientists believe that genetic mutations helped animals to evolve over thousands of years, helping them to fit into a given environment. Other genetic mutations are neither harmful nor helpful. Some genetic mutations are not harmful at present but make an organism more likely to develop cancer in the future if exposed to certain hazards in the environment.

Inherited or sporadic genetic mutations cannot be prevented. However, scientists have identified many environmental factors that may cause genetic mutations. Such mutations may increase the risk of cancer or directly cause cancer. Except for the first one, aging, people can do a lot to decrease their cancer risk. Known causes of cancer include:

• Aging: The older a person is, the greater the risk of developing cancer.

- Tobacco: Smoking tobacco is a recognized cause of cancer, especially lung cancer.
- Alcohol: The long-term use of alcohol can lead to cancer of the mouth, the throat, and the larynx.
- Chemicals: A number of chemicals and metals (such as benzene, cadmium, and pesticides) increase the risk for cancer. Painters, construction workers, and chemical factory workers may have an increased risk of cancer.
- Asbestos: Inhaling particles of asbestos (once widely used as insulation) can cause lung cancer.
- Bacteria: The bacteria *Helicobacter pylori* found in some people's stomachs can cause stomach cancer.
- Viruses: The hepatitis B virus can cause liver cancer. The human papillomavirus causes some forms of cervical cancer. There are vaccines that greatly decrease the risk for infection by these viruses.
- Ultraviolet radiation: The ultraviolet radiation found in sunlight is the primary cause of skin cancer.

Asbestos miners often suffered from lung cancer from inhaling particles of the mineral. This is a scene at an asbestos mine in the 1950s, before the asbestos link to cancer was discovered.

USA TODAY

www.usatoday.com

USA TODAY

Life
SECTION D

September 12, 2005

From the Pages of USA TODAY

Proven steps to a longer life:
For most people, better health can come with simple changes

Millions of Americans take steps to reduce their risk of heart disease, such as taking cholesterol-lowering drugs and watching the salt in their diets.

But most people don't know how to protect themselves from cancer, says Karen Collins, nutrition adviser to the American Institute for Cancer Research. Many people worry about possible environmental causes of cancer, such as pollution and food additives, but are unaware of proven ways to reduce their cancer risk, such as exercising and eating more vegetables, Collins says.

According to the American Cancer Society, about one-third of all cancer deaths—186,000 lives a year—could be prevented if people were more active and ate better. Parents can help their children avoid cancer as well by encouraging healthy habits from birth, says Carolyn Runowicz, president-elect of the Cancer Society and co-author of *The Answer to Cancer*.

People with a strong family history of a type of cancer might want to consider additional steps to stay healthy, such as being screened at younger ages, Runowicz says. Though there is no way to prevent all cancers, experts agree that for most people a handful of small changes greatly increases the odds of living a longer, healthier life.

Stay out of the sun: Keep children covered up. Up to 80% of lifetime sun

WHAT'S UP WITH ULTRAVIOLET RADIATION?

Earth could not exist without sunlight. The sun gives us light, warms our world, and provides energy for plants and animals to grow. Visible light—the light that we can see—is only one part of the electromagnetic spectrum. The electromagnetic spectrum contains gamma rays, X-rays, ultraviolet rays, infrared rays, radar, FM radio exposure occurs by age 18, says Runow-icz. She recommends staying out of the sun at midday, seeking shade, covering, using sunscreen that blocks both UVA and UVB radiation, and using SPF 15 lip balm.

Get your vitamins: To reduce the risk of colon cancer, strive for 1,500 milligrams of calcium and 400 micrograms of folic acid a day, either through diet or supplements.

Use alcohol in moderation: Heavy drinking contributes to oral, esophageal and liver cancers, says Ralph Coates, asso-ciate director for science in the Centers for Disease Control and Prevention's division of cancer prevention and control. Women should consume no more than one drink a day and men should stop at two.

Avoid tobacco: Cigarette smoking causes at least 30% of all cancer deaths. It causes tumors of the lungs, larynx, mouth, throat, esophagus, bladder, pancreas, liver, cervix, kidney, stomach, colon, rectum, and leuke-mia, the American Cancer Society says. It's never too late to stop. Ten years after giving up cigarettes, a person's risk of dying from lung cancer is 50% lower than if he or she had kept smoking.

Eat more fruits and vegetables: Diets centered on fruits and vegetables help protect against cancers of the lung, mouth, esophagus, stomach and colon, the American Cancer Society says. Groups such as the American Institute for Cancer Research encourage people to eats lots of different plant foods, because they might work best in combination.

Floss: Brushing and flossing might indirectly help protect against oral cancers by preventing gum disease, which might increase the risk of oral cancers, especially in people whose mouths have been dam-aged by drinking or smoking.

Cut back on meat: Meats such as hot dogs and bacon might increase the risk of colon cancer, according to an article published in the *Journal of the American Medical Association*. People who ate the most red and processed meat had a 30% higher risk of colon cancer and 40% greater risk of rectal cancer compared with those who consumed the least. People whose diets were rich in poultry and fish were 30% less likely to develop colon cancer.

Stay tuned: Doctors are learning more every day about ways to prevent cancer. People should talk to their doctors about ways to address their individual risks.

—Liz Szabo

waves, television waves, shortwave radio waves, and AM radio waves. We cannot see gamma rays or X-rays, radio waves, or TV waves. We cannot see ultraviolet rays or infrared rays. We can only see the narrow spectrum of waves that we call visible light. These waves are between ultraviolet and infrared rays in the spectrum. Visible light makes up the colors that we know—the colors of the rainbow.

Even though ultraviolet rays are invisible, they can irreparably damage a cell's DNA and lead to cancer. The rays are better known as ultraviolet radiation, or UV radiation. UV radiation literally breaks down DNA. This destruction produces a chemical that mutates genes. Genetic mutations allow cells to grow unchecked and to turn into cancer. There are three types of UV radiation: A, B, and C.

1. UVA penetrates more deeply into skin than the other types of UV. UVA is the main cause for wrinkling and premature aging of the skin. UVA also may cause melanoma and perhaps basal and squamous cell carcinomas. Most of the ultraviolet radiation that reaches Earth is UVA. It can pass through glass.

2. UVB penetrates only the top layers of the epidermis. UVB causes sunburn. It is the most damaging form of UV radiation. UVB is the primary cause of basal cell and squamous cell carcinoma. It cannot pass through glass.

3. UVC is absorbed by the ozone layer of the atmosphere before reaching Earth. The thinning of the ozone layer over some parts of the world may allow more UVC to reach us in the future. That could lead to more skin cancer.

Exposure to UV radiation depends on geography. Since the equator is the closest point to the sun on Earth, people who live at or near the equator receive the most sunlight and the most UV radiation. The indigenous people of Africa and the Aboriginal people of Australia have dark skin, which helps minimize damage from UV radiation. Large numbers of fair-skinned Europeans immigrated to Australia in the nineteenth and twentieth centuries. These former Europeans have little protection against UV radiation. Australia has the highest rate of skin cancer in the world.

www.usatoday.com

News
SECTION A

September 26, 2003

From the Pages of USA TODAY

Antarctica ozone hole gets larger:
Affected area 2nd-largest ever recorded, report says

The size of the ozone hole over Antarctica is the second-largest ever recorded, federal researchers reported. The region of ozone-depleted air peaked in size over the South Pole on September 11, 2003, when it covered 10.9 million square miles [28 million square kilometers], an area larger than North America. It measures second in size to the 2000 ozone hole that grew to 11.5 million square miles [30 million sq. km].

The size of the ozone hole has been carefully watched for decades. Atmospheric ozone screens harmful ultraviolet rays from the sun, but it has been eroded by man-made chemicals such as chlorofluorocarbons. That has led to fears of increased skin cancers, especially if the hole expands over heavily populated areas.

The report on the near-record size of the hole by researchers from NASA, the National Oceanic and Atmospheric Administration, and the Naval Research Laboratory bolsters predictions that Earth faces sizable ozone holes for at least the next decade. Current projections are for ozone holes to linger over Antarctica until at least 2050.

A 1988 worldwide agreement gradually bans chlorine and bromine-based chemicals that strip ozone from the atmosphere. But the chemicals can linger for decades, causing damage even after they are no longer in use.

Some researchers have speculated that worldwide climate changes may worsen the Antarctic ozone hole and keep it around for more years than expected. Man-made "greenhouse" gases cool the stratosphere and may lead to more cloud formation there. That could generate even more ozone depletion.

—*Dan Vergano*

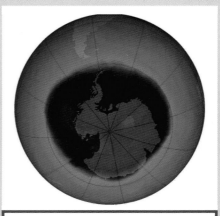

This colored satellite image shows the extent of the the ozone hole (dark blue) over Antarctica in 2009.

People who live or vacation at high altitudes also have an increased risk of skin cancer. UV radiation increases 4 to 5 percent for every 1,000 feet (300 m) above sea level. Someone living high in the Rocky Mountains at an elevation of 8,000 feet (2,400 m) has a 32 to 40 percent higher risk of developing skin cancer than someone living at sea level in San Francisco, California.

Clouds offer no protection against UV radiation. People are as much at risk for skin damage on a cloudy day as on a sunny day. Being at the ocean, in a lake, or in a pool increases the risk for skin damage from UV radiation because sunlight reflects off the water.

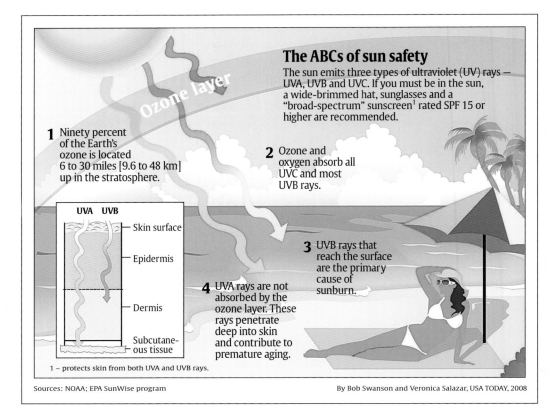

Ozone layer

The ABCs of sun safety

The sun emits three types of ultraviolet (UV) rays — UVA, UVB and UVC. If you must be in the sun, a wide-brimmed hat, sunglasses and a "broad-spectrum" sunscreen[1] rated SPF 15 or higher are recommended.

1 Ninety percent of the Earth's ozone is located 6 to 30 miles [9.6 to 48 km] up in the stratosphere.

2 Ozone and oxygen absorb all UVC and most UVB rays.

UVA UVB

Skin surface

Epidermis

Dermis

Subcutane-ous tissue

3 UVB rays that reach the surface are the primary cause of sunburn.

4 UVA rays are not absorbed by the ozone layer. These rays penetrate deep into skin and contribute to premature aging.

1 – protects skin from both UVA and UVB rays.

Sources: NOAA; EPA SunWise program

By Bob Swanson and Veronica Salazar, USA TODAY, 2008

It's like being hit with a double whammy. Both direct and reflected sunlight hit people who are boating or swimming. The same thing happens to people lying on a light-colored sandy beach.

We can greatly reduce our chance for developing skin cancer by protecting ourselves from excessive amounts of sunlight. Yet not all people know how to protect themselves, or if they do know, they fail to do so. Those people are likely to develop the most common types of skin cancer, basal cell carcinoma and squamous cell carcinoma.

When Anne's biopsy came back, it showed that the dark "freckle" was a melanoma, the most serious form of skin cancer. Anne's doctor was able to remove all of it. "Luckily, this was a wake-up call, and not a death sentence," she said. "Since then, I've stayed out of the sun and use sunscreen religiously."

"Watching out for the sun isn't the first thing that springs to a teen's mind when she goes to the beach," Anne said. "Learn about sun block, SPF [sun protection factor], wear a hat that shades your ears, and make sunglasses part of your wardrobe. This helps to prevent burns and skin cancer. The bonus for taking care of your skin now is that when you are older, you'll look years younger than you are. People will comment on what beautiful skin you have. Who can resist that?"

CHAPTER THREE

BASAL CELL AND SQUAMOUS CELL CARCINOMA

Skin cancers are classified as melanomas—the most serious form of skin cancer—and non-melanomas. Non-melanoma skin cancer includes basal cell carcinoma and squamous cell carcinoma. Carcinoma is the name for a cancer that starts in the skin's epithelial cells. Non-melanoma skin cancer is easy to treat and cure when it is detected early. Even so, an estimated one thousand to two thousand Americans die each year from non-melanoma skin cancer.

Because non-melanoma skin cancers are not reported to cancer registries, we cannot be certain how many people develop them. Experts estimate that more than one million Americans get basal cell or squamous cell carcinomas each year. In addition, many more people develop the precancerous condition known as actinic keratosis that can lead to skin cancer.

PRECANCER: ACTINIC KERATOSIS

"I have a lot of freckles," says Alexandria Hudson, a senior at a high school in Texas. "No matter how hard I try, I cannot tan. I burn. I blister. Recently, I talked myself into lying out by the pool for an hour—only an hour—without sunscreen. I spent the following two weeks nursing blisters the size of golf balls." Alexandria saw a dermatologist for her severe sunburn.

"I finally realized what I was doing to myself. Having three quarter-sized sunspots cut out of my abdomen to be tested for cancer was a rude awakening." The idea of a perfect tan, she said, "means little when you're dealing with the removal of precancerous sunspots." Alexandria's dermatologist told her that less than half of all teens use sunscreen.

"Having only one blistering burn in adolescence more than doubles a person's chance of getting skin cancer later in life," she said.

A sunspot is a common name for actinic keratosis. The words mean: "a thick, scaly growth caused by sunlight." That's a good description. Frequent or intense exposure to ultraviolet radiation is the main cause of actinic keratoses (plural for keratosis). They are so common that one out every six Americans will develop at least one. Actinic keratoses occur more frequently among older people, but as Alexandria found out, they can develop at any age.

Actinic keratoses may be gray, pink, red, or the same color as a person's skin. They start as flat, scaly areas. The spots later turn hard and wartlike. They can burn or itch and may be gritty or rough, with a surface that feels like sandpaper. It may be easier to feel actinic keratoses with your fingers than to see them. They can be any size, but are usually less than 1 inch (2.5 centimeters) in diameter.

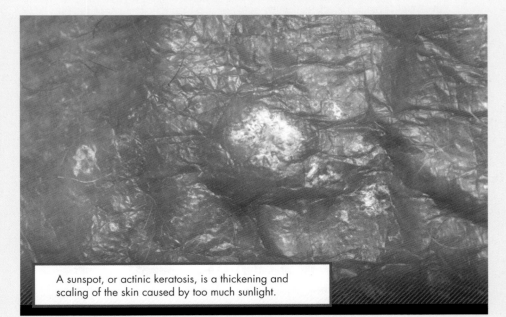

A sunspot, or actinic keratosis, is a thickening and scaling of the skin caused by too much sunlight.

Actinic keratoses often appear on the face and sometimes on the lips. Other common places are on the scalp, the ears, the backs of the hands, and the forearms, all places frequently exposed to the sun.

Actinic keratoses sometimes heal on their own, but they may return after additional sun exposure. Any new skin change warrants a visit to the doctor but especially one that's painful, itches or burns, oozes or bleeds, becomes scaly or crusty, or changes in size, shape, or color. An actinic keratosis is considered precancerous—not yet cancer but with the possibility of turning into cancer.

Dermatologists remove actinic keratoses by burning, freezing, or cutting them off. They can also use medications that cause the skin to peel. Removal of actinic keratoses costs more than $1 billion each year in the United States.

Without removal, between 5 and 20 percent of actinic keratoses turn into squamous cell carcinoma, the second most common form of skin cancer. In 2009 scientists at Brown University in Rhode Island discovered that actinic keratosis may also turn into basal cell carcinoma. Researchers studied over one thousand people with actinic keratoses. Two-thirds of the people who later developed squamous cell carcinoma could trace their cancer to actinic keratoses. One-third of the people who developed basal cell carcinoma traced their cancer to actinic keratoses. People with a long history of sun exposure may have dozens of actinic keratoses. These sunspots should be examined by a doctor.

BASAL CELL CARCINOMA

When Jerry was a child, he and his family often headed out on the weekends to Jones Beach on Long Island, New York. "Everyone else in my family got a nice tan. I always got a sunburn, even when the sky was overcast. I reluctantly allowed my mother to apply a thin layer of tanning lotion on me, but it never helped me to tan."

When Jerry was twenty-five, he noticed a red, pimple-sized spot on his face that started to crust over and bleed. That sent him to a dermatologist. The doctor used an electric needle to remove the spot and told Jerry that it was basal cell carcinoma. "Ten years later, another one showed up on my cheek. Then another. And another." Over the past thirty years, doctors have removed at least twenty basal cell carcinomas from Jerry's face and chest and a few dozen actinic keratoses as well. "I'd tell young people to limit their sun time, to wear sunscreen, and to avoid tanning booths. You'll thank yourselves later."

Basal cell carcinoma originates in the stratum basale, the very thin layer of cells that lies at the lowest level of the epidermis. The stratum basale contains the basal cells that continually make new skin cells. Basal cell carcinoma is the most common form of skin cancer. About 75 to 80 percent of all skin cancers are basal cell carcinomas. It is so common that one out of every five Americans will develop at least one of these skin cancers during their lifetime.

Basal cell carcinoma used to be found mostly in middle-aged and elderly people. More recently it is being found in younger people too.

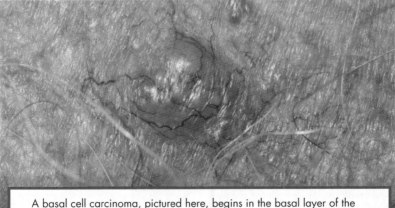

A basal cell carcinoma, pictured here, begins in the basal layer of the skin, where new skin cells form. It is the most common type of skin cancer.

Rates of basal cell carcinoma have tripled among women younger than forty. Even so, more men than women develop basal cell carcinoma. Risk factors for basal cell carcinoma include the following:

- Exposure to the sun's ultraviolet radiation, especially during childhood and adolescence
- Excessive use of tanning beds
- Fair skin, red or blond hair, green or blue eyes
- Older age
- Presence of a weakened immune system as a result of treatment for other cancers, organ transplant, or diagnosis of HIV/AIDS
- Genetic susceptibility, especially mutations in the *PATCHED* genes or tumor suppressor genes (genes that inhibit tumor growth)
- Exposure to certain pesticides and industrial chemicals in the workplace
- Exposure to other types of radiation received during medical treatment, such as for the skin condition psoriasis
- Male gender. Men are twice as likely to get basal cell carcinoma as women. Men have more skin cancer of all types than women. They spend up to ten hours more each week in the sun than women and are much less likely to use sunscreen. Men work outdoors more and play outdoor sports more often than women. Men often take off their shirts when outdoors, leading to an increased risk for cancers of the back, the chest, and the shoulders. They also have less hair than women to cover their ears and scalps, which may result in more skin cancer in those areas. If men wear hats outdoors, they are likely to wear a baseball-type cap, which fails to protect the neck and most of the face. Finally, men are less likely to visit a doctor for a routine skin screening or for a seemingly minor problem such as a new spot on the skin.

www.usatoday.com

USA TODAY
Life
SECTION D

August 10, 2005

From the Pages of USA TODAY

Milder skin cancers becoming more common among young
Consequences could lie ahead

More young people appear to be developing the most common types of skin cancer, a change that could herald a dramatic increase in the cost and suffering caused by the disease.

Mayo Clinic researchers studied basal and squamous cell carcinomas, cancers that are almost always curable and that together afflict more than one million Americans a year, according to an article published in the *Journal of the American Medical Association*. The cancers, caused largely by overexposure to ultraviolet light from the sun, usually develop in older people who have spent many years outdoors.

In the study, doctors focused on people under 40 years old in one Minnesota county. From 1976–1979 to 2000–2003, the combined rate of the two skin cancers grew from 19 cases per 100,000 people to 33 per 100,000—a 74% increase. Although up to 90% of such cancers typically appear on the head and neck, doctors in the study found 40% of skin cancers on other parts of the body, a change that probably reflects the effect of excessive sunbathing.

Doctors studied only one county, where most people are white. But researchers say their findings probably indicate an increased rate of skin cancer nationwide, at least among Caucasians, says the study's lead author, Leslie Christenson, a Mayo Clinic dermatologic surgeon.

The study suggests skin cancer could become a much larger public health problem in the decades ahead, says Darrell Rigel, former president of the American Academy of Dermatology. About half of people who develop a basal cell carcinoma develop at least one more, suggesting that these young people could be burdened by cancer for the next 30 to 40 years.

Christenson says it's possible that some of the increase in basal and squamous cell carcinomas could be caused by increased screenings. But tanning probably plays a more important role. Basal and squamous cell carcinomas can be disfiguring, even if they rarely spread or turn fatal, Christenson says. According to the American Cancer Society, these cancers kill about 1,000 to 2,000 people a year. "For a preventable cancer, that's too bad," Christenson says.

—Liz Szabo

USA TODAY

Basal cell carcinomas are normally painless and grow very slowly. They are most commonly found on the face, the chest, the arms, and the back. Occasionally basal cell carcinomas grow on the eyelids, especially the lower eyelids. They may look like irregular red scaly areas spread across the skin, or they may be raised and pink to red in color. They can be flat, shiny, waxy, or transparent. Sometimes the spots contain areas of blue, brown, or black coloration. As a basal cell carcinoma grows larger, it develops its own blood supply. These abnormal-looking blood vessels are often visible.

If they are injured, basal cell carcinomas can bleed or become sore. Large basal cell carcinomas may crust over or ooze. It may be difficult to tell a simple skin injury from a basal cell carcinoma. Injuries to the skin heal in a month or two. Basal cell carcinomas do not heal.

It is extremely rare for basal cell carcinomas to metastasize. They spread to nearby lymph nodes or to distant parts of the body in less than 1 percent of people with basal cell carcinoma. However, left untreated, basal cell carcinomas can spread to nearby tissues and destroy them. They can even invade the bone that lies under the cancer. After treatment, basal cell carcinoma may recur in the same place. About half of the people who have had one basal cell carcinoma will have another one within five years.

SQUAMOUS CELL CARCINOMA

Ginger calls herself the SCC (squamous cell carcinoma) queen because she's had two squamous cell carcinomas removed. "I grew up in a beach town in Southern California. My mother took me and my brothers to the beach nearly every day in the summer. We also went camping in the desert several times each year. None of us ever used sunscreen or tried to protect our skin in any way. We just didn't know any better.

"My first SCC was in the middle of my back. It started out as an irregular, rough, raised area that bothered me because my clothing rubbed against it. The spot would occasionally bleed. I'd been seeing a dermatologist for several years because of numerous basal cell carcinomas, but this was different. It was big enough that it required several stitches to close the wound after the doctor removed it. My second SCC was on the back of my thigh. Every time I bumped the spot, it would bleed." Ginger's squamous cell carcinomas developed many years after the areas had been exposed to sun. "My doctor predicts that I'll get more of them," she says.

Squamous cell carcinoma originates in squamous cells of the epidermis, the cells that make up most of the epidermis. This form of skin cancer also may develop from existing actinic keratoses. About 15 to 20 percent of skin cancers are squamous cell carcinoma, making it the second most common form of skin cancer. About 250,000 Americans develop squamous cell carcinoma each year.

The risk factors for squamous cell carcinoma are similar to those for

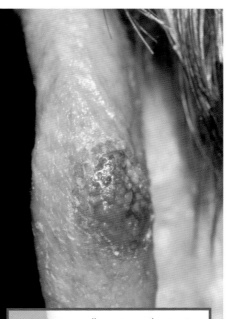

Squamous cell carcinoma begins in the squamous cells of the epidermis, and it often develops from an actinic keratosis. It is the second most common form of skin cancer. This cancer appeared on the edge of a man's ear.

basal cell carcinoma and include the following:

- Frequent exposure to the sun's ultraviolet radiation, especially among outdoor workers and people who often participate in outdoor activities
- Excessive use of tanning beds
- Male gender. Squamous cell carcinoma is about three times more common in men than in women.
- Older age
- Fair skin; red or blond hair; green, gray, or blue eyes
- Areas of skin with constant irritation due to burns, scars, and chronic sores
- Skin previously exposed to radiation treatment for medical conditions
- Infection with the human papillomavirus (which also causes cervical cancer)
- Previous basal cell carcinomas

Squamous cell carcinomas can occur on any area of the skin but most commonly are found in places with frequent sun exposure, such as the top of the ears, the lower lip, the face, the legs, the neck, the hands, the arms, and on bald scalps. Like basal cell carcinomas, they also can be found on the eyelids.

It can be difficult to tell skin lesions apart. Actinic keratoses, basal cell carcinomas, and squamous cell carcinomas may be similar in appearance. Usually a doctor must perform a biopsy and examine the abnormal cells under a microscope to confirm the type of lesion. Many squamous cell carcinomas have an irregular shape. They are slow growing but often crust over and may occasionally bleed. They can look like warts; open sores that do not heal; persistent, scaly, red, irregular patches; or raised growths with a central depression that occasionally bleeds.

Skin Type Categories

People with skin types I, II, and III are most likely to develop skin cancer.

Skin Type	Skin Color/Eyes/Hair	Effects of UV Radiation Exposure
I	very white or pale skin, blue or green eyes, red hair, many freckles	always burns, never tans, extremely sun-sensitive skin
II	white skin; blue, hazel, green eyes; red, blond or light brown hair; some freckles	usually burns, tans poorly, very sun-sensitive skin
III	fair or light brown skin; any eye color but often brown	burns moderately but can tan, sun-sensitive skin
IV	light brown or olive skin, brown eyes, often with brown hair	burns minimally, tans easily, minimally sun-sensitive skin
V	brown skin, dark brown hair and eyes	rarely burns, tans easily, sun-insensitive skin
VI	black or very dark brown skin, very dark eyes and hair	rarely or never burns, tans easily, sun-insensitive skin

Squamous cell carcinomas are more aggressive than basal cell carcinomas. They tend to grow faster and may invade the fatty tissue below the hypodermis. They can metastasize and travel to distant parts of the body, although this is uncommon. About 2 percent of people who develop squamous cell carcinomas end up with metastases. This happens more often in people with weakened immune systems. If squamous cell carcinomas are removed, nearly one in ten will return.

As many as two thousand Americans die each year of non-melanoma skin cancer. Yet basal cell and squamous cell carcinoma can be completely cured when treated early.

TREATMENT FOR ACTINIC KERATOSIS AND NON-MELANOMA SKIN CANCERS

Most family doctors can identify an abnormal skin lesion. If the doctor suspects an actinic keratosis or skin cancer, he or she may send the patient to a dermatologist. Dermatologists are trained to recognize and treat all kinds of skin diseases, from acne to cancer.

MAKING THE DIAGNOSIS

Some people see a dermatologist only if their family doctor recommends it. Other people with a long history of sun exposure and skin damage have a yearly skin checkup with their dermatologist. The doctor starts by taking a history. He or she will ask the patient about past sun exposure. For example, where did the patient grow up and how much time was spent in the sun or working outdoors? The doctor may ask about family history of skin cancer or if the patient has ever been exposed to other conditions that might cause skin cancer.

Next, the doctor does a physical exam. He or she examines the size, the shape, the color, and the texture of the skin lesion. The doctor will ask if the patient experienced any bleeding or crusting of the area. The doctor will check nearby lymph nodes to see if they are firmer than usual. This sometimes indicates that the skin cancer has spread to the lymph nodes.

Lymph nodes are an important part of our immune system. We have between five hundred and six hundred lymph nodes scattered throughout our bodies. Clusters of lymph nodes are found under the arms, in the groin, around the neck, and inside the chest and the abdomen. These bean-shaped organs range in size from 0.25 to 0.50 inches (0.6 to 1.3 cm) to 0.50 to 1.0 inches (1 to 2 cm). Lymph nodes are connected by lymph vessels that carry lymphatic fluid in much the same way that blood vessels carry blood.

Lymph nodes help to filter out bacteria. For example, if you ever had strep throat, you might remember feeling "swollen glands" along the sides of your neck. Those swollen glands were actually lymph nodes doing their job. Lymph nodes contain large numbers of white blood cells and other cells that make up the immune system. When lymph nodes filter out bacteria, the immune system goes to work to kill the bacteria. Lymph nodes also catch cancer cells that travel from a tumor.

After checking the lymph nodes, the doctor may use a piece of equipment called a dermatoscope, a lighted magnifying glass to closely examine the lesion. Doctors use a system known as staging to determine how widespread a cancer is. If she suspects skin cancer, she may assign a stage to the cancer. The stage also indicates whether the cancer has metastasized to other parts of the body.

In basal cell carcinoma, stages are only assigned to large lesions. Squamous cell carcinomas, which have a greater risk of metastasis, are usually staged. Once the doctor knows the cancer's stage, the doctor can plan treatment. A biopsy can help the doctor to determine the stage of the cancer.

Stages of Non-melanoma Skin Cancers

Stage	Description
0	The cancer involves only the epidermis and has not spread to the dermis.
I	The cancer is no larger than 2 centimeters (less than 1 inch). It does not invade deeply into muscle, cartilage, or bone and has not spread to lymph nodes or other organs.
II	The cancer is larger than 2 centimeters (about 1 inch or more). It does not invade deeply into muscle, cartilage, or bone and has not spread to lymph nodes or other organs.
III	The cancer has grown into tissues beneath the skin (such as muscle, bone, or cartilage), and/or it has spread to nearby lymph nodes.
IV	The cancer can be any size and may or may not have spread to local lymph nodes. It has spread to other organs such as the lungs or the brain.

Source: American Cancer Society

BIOPSY AND SURGICAL TREATMENT

The dermatologist will need to biopsy most skin lesions, even if she does not suspect squamous cell carcinoma. Dermatologists can perform biopsies with a minimal risk of scarring. In most cases, the doctor sends the tissue obtained from a biopsy to a pathologist, a doctor who specializes in looking at human tissue to determine if it is cancerous. There are several types of biopsies:

- Shave biopsy: The doctor numbs the skin with a local anesthetic much like the dentist numbs a tooth before fixing a cavity. The doctor then shaves off the top layers of the skin—the epidermis and the top part of the dermis.
- Punch biopsy: After numbing the skin, the doctor uses a biopsy tool that looks like a tiny round cookie cutter. The tool is punched into the skin and rotated to obtain a sample that goes through all layers of the skin and into the upper part of the subcutis.
- Incisional biopsy: The doctor cuts out part of the lesion or tumor.
- Excisional biopsy: The doctor cuts out the entire lesion or tumor.
- Lymph node biopsy: The doctor may use a very thin needle to remove a tiny bit of tissue from a swollen lymph node. In some cases, an entire lymph node may be removed under local anesthesia and sent to a pathologist.

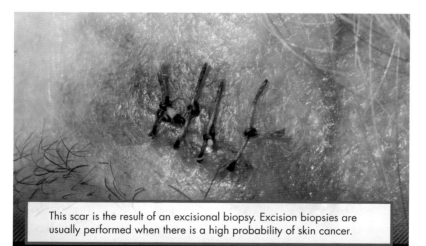

This scar is the result of an excisional biopsy. Excision biopsies are usually performed when there is a high probability of skin cancer.

Treatment begins after the biopsy confirms that the lesion is an actinic keratosis, a basal cell carcinoma, or a squamous cell carcinoma. There are several kinds of surgeries used to treat skin cancer. Many will leave a scar. The size of the scar depends on the size and depth of the cancer. Plastic surgeons can correct a scar if the patient finds it unacceptable.

Most often the doctor will use a simple excision. In this procedure, the tumor is cut out along with some surrounding normal skin. The remaining skin is carefully stitched together over the wound. The doctor will often scrape away smaller basal and squamous cell carcinomas with an instrument called a curette. Then she will treat the skin with an electric needle to destroy any remaining cancer cells and to stop bleeding. If cancers have spread to nearby lymph nodes, the doctor must remove the lymph nodes as well as the tumor.

Some surgeons are trained in the special type of skin cancer surgery called Mohs surgery. With this technique, the surgeon removes a very thin layer of skin and examines it immediately under a microscope. If he sees cancer cells, he removes another layer of skin and examines it. This goes on until the surgeon reaches a layer of the skin that is completely normal. While Mohs surgery can take several hours, it saves more healthy skin and leaves less scarring than other surgeries. This time-consuming surgery is usually reserved for skin cancers on the face.

Caryn, whom we met in chapter 1, had Mohs surgeries performed on squamous cell carcinomas on her temple and nose. *"Mohs takes a long time,"* she said, *"but it's a wonderful procedure. It took nearly seven hours for me, but you emerge knowing that all the cancer has been removed without removing large areas of normal skin. This means much less scarring. Despite having two Mohs surgeries on my nose, I have no obvious scars."*

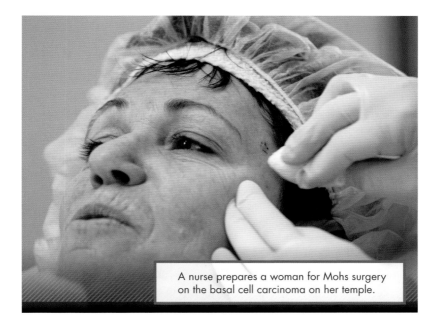

A nurse prepares a woman for Mohs surgery on the basal cell carcinoma on her temple.

Some non-melanoma skin cancers are so large that the nearby skin cannot be stretched to cover the surgical site. They may require a skin graft. In this procedure, the surgeon removes a portion of a person's normal skin from another part of the body and stitches it over the surgical site. For example, a small piece of skin from the abdomen or back may be used to cover an incision on the face.

MEDICAL TREATMENT

Many actinic keratoses and small non-melanoma skin cancers are treated with cryosurgery. The doctor applies liquid nitrogen that freezes the actinic keratosis or the cancer. Nitrogen is normally a gas that makes up part of our atmosphere. However, in a liquid form, nitrogen is extremely cold, about -320°F (-200°C). The tissue does not die because it is frozen—it dies as it thaws out. It blisters and crusts over. The area heals in one month to two months and may leave a small scar.

Photodynamic therapy is another method dermatologists use to remove skin cancers. In this treatment, doctors apply a photosensitizing (light sensitive) drug directly to the skin cancer. Then the doctor directs a specific wavelength of light to the site to kill the cancer cells. This works well on basal cell carcinomas and actinic keratoses. The doctor may also inject a photosensitizing drug into the patient's bloodstream. The drug collects inside the cancer cells and remains in them longer than in healthy cells. In a day or two, the patient returns to the doctor's office to receive the light treatment that kills the cancer cells.

Laser surgery uses a focused, high-powered beam of light to pulverize a cancer. Laser surgery is used for a small squamous cell carcinoma that has not spread and for very superficial basal cell carcinomas. Laser surgery causes less pain, bleeding, and scarring than regular surgery. The downside is that laser treatments may need to be repeated, while a surgical treatment is usually permanent.

The doctor may use radiation therapy after surgery to kill any remaining cancer cells or on skin cancers that have returned. The patient may need several treatments to completely destroy a large tumor. Radiation therapy is more often used to treat cancers such as breast cancer, colon cancer, and other cancers of the internal organs.

Chemotherapy, which involves giving very powerful medications to people with cancer to kill cancer cells, may have serious side effects. People with skin cancer can receive local applications of chemotherapy drugs with minimal problems. One common medication used in the treatment of skin cancer is fluorouracil—known as 5-FU. The doctor applies the 5-FU directly to the skin in a cream form. Because the cream cannot penetrate very deeply, it is often used to treat actinic keratoses. It can be used to treat both basal and squamous cell carcinomas if they are on or near the surface.

Immune response modifiers are medications that stimulate the body's own immune system to react to a skin lesion and destroy it. One of these medications is a topical cream named imiquimod (brand name Aldara). This medication is used to treat actinic keratoses and some basal cell carcinomas. Interferon, another immune response modifier, is a version of a natural immune system protein made in a laboratory. Interferon can be injected directly into a large tumor to help the body's immune system fight the cancer.

A doctor has a lot to consider when treating a patient with actinic keratoses or non-melanoma skin cancers. The doctor will take into account the size, the depth, and the location of the lesion to decide what treatment will work best. For example, people tend to have several actinic keratoses at a time. For those people, the doctor may use cryosurgery and topical creams, such as 5-FU or imiquimod, so that large areas of skin can be treated at the same time. A patient with a big squamous cell carcinoma will likely require excision and possibly a skin graft. While surgeries can leave scars, topical creams may cause days of discomfort; swelling; and reddened, weeping areas.

People who have had an actinic keratosis or a basal cell or squamous cell carcinoma are very likely to have more in the future. These people often have skin that has been damaged by many years of overexposure to the sun's ultraviolet radiation. Doctors will recommend they return to the office for an annual skin examination. People with a history of skin cancer or actinic keratoses should learn how to examine their own skin between medical visits.

CHAPTER FOUR

MELANOMA

A couple of times a week, after working out at the gym, twenty-two-year-old Nate Schwegman dropped by the tanning salon and sizzled in the tanning bed. His fair, freckled skin would first burn, then peel, and then burn again, before turning a nice bronze. "I might as well look good when I'm young," he said. "I don't care if I wrinkle when I'm old."

One day in the bathroom mirror, he noticed a black mark on his back. It was a little smaller than a dime. "It almost looked like a scab," he said. He assumed that it was a mole and didn't think about it again for nearly a year. It wasn't until the spot started to bleed that Nate finally saw a dermatologist. A biopsy showed it was advanced melanoma. "I flipped out," he said. "I didn't think it was ever going to happen to me."

Remember Hippocrates of Ancient Greece, the father of medicine, who named cancer after crabs? He also described melanoma as a fatal black tumor with metastases. In 1806 French doctor Rene Laennec described and named the tumors, *la melanose,* from the Greek word *melan* (meaning "black"). It was a fitting name. Many melanomas are black in color.

Melanoma is less common than many other kinds of cancer. According to the American Cancer Society, melanoma accounts for less than 5 percent of all skin cancers. About one out of every fifty people of northern European ancestry will develop melanoma. Melanoma is most often a cancer of light-skinned people. But people with darker skin can get it as well. About one in two hundred Hispanics will get melanoma, as will one in a thousand African Americans. Compare those numbers to two very common cancers: about one out of eight

Melanomas, like this one, have become the most common kind of cancer in women twenty-five to twenty-nine years old.

women will develop breast cancer during her life, and an estimated one in six men will develop prostate cancer.

About 68,700 Americans were diagnosed with melanoma in 2009. That same year, an estimated 8,650 people died from melanoma. Compared to the number of people who die from cancers of the lung, the colon, the breast, and the prostate, that isn't a lot. But melanoma is becoming more common. Twice as many people develop melanoma than did so thirty years ago. It has become the most common cancer in young women between twenty-five and twenty-nine years old, and the second most common among women aged thirty to thirty-four (breast cancer is first).

THE NASTY NEVI

Melanoma starts in the melanocytes. These are the cells in the basal layer of the epidermis that produce the pigment melanin. The melanocytes of people with darker skin naturally produce more melanin than the melanocytes in people with lighter skin. Melanin absorbs some of sunlight's UV radiation. This helps to protect the DNA in skin cells from damage. Melanocytes also produce extra melanin when skin is exposed to the sun. A sun tan is nothing more than a temporary increase in melanin. While some people admire how they look with a tan, tanned skin is a sign of sun damage.

Sometimes melanocytes clump together to form moles. Moles are actually small, benign tumors and are very common. Most people have ten to forty moles on their body. They may be pink, tan, brown, or a color very close to the person's normal skin color. They can be flat or raised. Moles are usually round or oval and smaller than the top of a pencil eraser. They are seldom present at birth but begin to appear in children, teens, and young adults.

Nevus is the medical name for a mole (nevi is plural). Most nevi never cause any problems. But sometimes moles grow darker or bigger or change shape. Doctors call these abnormal moles dysplastic nevi. They look a little bit like normal moles, but they also look a little bit like melanomas. Dysplastic nevi are usually larger than

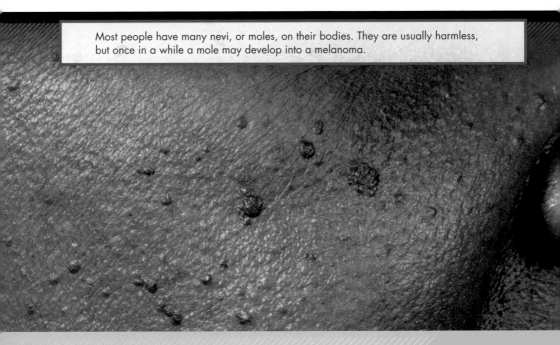

Most people have many nevi, or moles, on their bodies. They are usually harmless, but once in a while a mole may develop into a melanoma.

regular moles. They may appear in areas that are exposed to the sun. They can also appear in areas of skin that are normally covered by clothing.

A small number of dysplastic nevi turn into melanomas. Most do not. Many people who get melanomas never have a dysplastic nevus. Even so, if a person has several of these abnormal moles or if the person has family members with them, the risk for developing melanoma is increased. Doctors watch dysplastic nevi closely. If a nevus changes—grows larger or darker—the doctor may recommend surgery to remove it before it has a chance to turn into melanoma.

OTHER RISK FACTORS FOR MELANOMA

A risk factor is something that affects your chance of getting a disease such as cancer. For example, smoking is a huge risk factor for getting lung cancer. Ultraviolet radiation is a risk factor for getting skin cancer. But having a risk factor does not mean you will get a disease. It means that your chances of getting it are higher than someone without the same risk factor. Still, many people get cancer without having any known risk factors. Others who have one or more risk factors may never get cancer.

Scientists have found several risk factors that make a person more likely to develop melanoma.

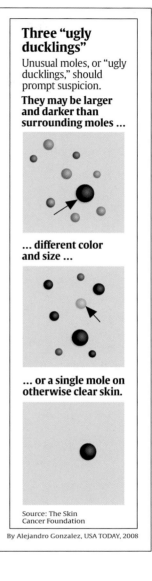

Three "ugly ducklings"

Unusual moles, or "ugly ducklings," should prompt suspicion.

They may be larger and darker than surrounding moles ...

... different color and size ...

... or a single mole on otherwise clear skin.

Source: The Skin Cancer Foundation

By Alejandro Gonzalez, USA TODAY, 2008

- Ultraviolet radiation: Melanomas often arise from too much sun exposure. The ultraviolet radiation in sunlight damages a cell's DNA so badly that the cell can no longer repair itself. The amount of UV radiation that reaches the skin depends on time in the sun, whether the skin was protected, and the location of exposure (beach, water, mountains, etc.). UV radiation is also found in the light from tanning beds and sunlamps.

- Sunburn: Having a severe, blistering sunburn as a child or teen increases the risk of melanoma.

- Moles: Having more than fifty ordinary moles or more than a few dysplastic nevi increases the risk for melanoma.

- Coloring: As with other skin cancers, people who have fair skin, light hair and eyes, and a tendency to freckle are at increased risk for melanoma. They have much less natural protective melanin than people with darker skin.

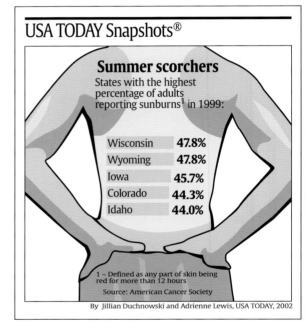

USA TODAY Snapshots®

Summer scorchers
States with the highest percentage of adults reporting sunburns[1] in 1999:

Wisconsin	**47.8%**
Wyoming	**47.8%**
Iowa	**45.7%**
Colorado	**44.3%**
Idaho	**44.0%**

1 – Defined as any part of skin being red for more than 12 hours

Source: American Cancer Society

By Jillian Duchnowski and Adrienne Lewis, USA TODAY, 2002

- Family history: The risk of melanoma is greater for people with a first-degree relative (parent, sibling, or child) who had it. About 10 percent of people with melanoma have a family history of it. Some families have genetic mutations that

www.usatoday.com

Money
SECTION B

June 16, 2008

From the Pages of USA TODAY

Sun protection for kids gets more intense
Marketers respond to parental anxiety

If your kids get sunburned, they're not toast, you are. Or so a new wave of sun-protection-product marketers are convincing many, particularly older and affluent, parents.

Former top sun-block-protection levels of SPF 50 seem almost outdated with some new sun blocks boasting levels up to SPF 70. Special sun-blocking sunglasses for kids are high fashion, as are swimwear and apparel that block sun rays. Sales of sun covers for baby strollers have quadrupled the past five years.

Sun-protection gear for kids may soon be as common as bicycle helmets, says Stacy DeBroff, CEO of Mom Central Consulting. "A kid's sunburn has become one step away from calling the department of social services."

The driver: heightened parental anxiety over the effects of sun exposure on kids. Parents worry over ozone depletion strengthening the sun's damaging rays. What's more, some baby boomers, finding out they have skin cancer, are eager to protect their kids and grandkids.

One blistering childhood sunburn doubles the chances of developing melanoma later in life, the Skin Cancer Foundation reports. A baby's skin is thinner than an adult's, so a baby will burn far more easily, the American Academy of Pediatrics says. The risk for melanoma doubles for those who have had five or more sunburns at any age.

—Bruce Horovitz

increase their risk of melanoma. Scientists are discovering new mutations that further increase the risk.

- Previous melanoma: A person who has had a melanoma in the past is more likely to get another in the future than a person who has never had a melanoma.

USA TODAY

www.usatoday.com
Life
SECTION D

May 1, 2006

From the Pages of USA TODAY

Rooting out skin cancer
Melanomas aren't always found in the obvious places

Have you ever examined the back of your head? Do you even know what the soles of your feet look like? If not, maybe it's time to take a peek. Each year when springtime sun beckons us outside—dermatologists remind people to spend a few minutes examining their skin for signs of cancer.

Skin cancers, including dangerous melanomas, are closely linked to sun damage. Most arise on easily seen, frequently exposed areas of the skin, such as the face, limbs and trunk. But melanomas also can show up where the sun does not shine—between the buttocks, on the soles or the palms or between the toes, for example—or in areas that are hard to see, such as the scalp.

A good self-exam should include those areas, says dermatologist Stephen Stone,

- Immune system suppression: Anything that weakens the immune system increases the risk for melanoma. This includes having had an organ transplant, receiving chemotherapy for cancer, or being infected with HIV.
- Age: Even though melanoma is becoming more common in young people, the chance of developing it increases with age.
- Gender: Men have a higher rate of melanoma than women.
- Xeroderma pigmentosum (XP): XP is a very rare inherited defect of an enzyme, a body chemical, that normally repairs damaged DNA. People with XP can develop serious skin cancers at a very young age. In the United States, about one person in one million has XP.

president of the American Academy of Dermatology. "The so-called 'hidden' melanomas tend to be more advanced when we find them," he says, because people are less likely to notice them or recognize their danger.

Patti Good, 45, of Springfield, Illinois, wife and mother of three, says that for a year she felt a bump on the back of her head "and never thought anything about it" until a news article on the signs of melanoma "started my heart racing." She called her family doctor at once and within days was having surgeries to remove a large melanoma and 27 lymph nodes. The nodes were cancer-free, and after one year of interferon treatment plus eight years of careful screenings, Good has seen no further cancer signs.

Some rarer hidden melanomas are found beneath nails; on mucous membranes lining the nose, mouth, vagina, anus, urinary tract or esophagus; and on the eyelid or eyeball. Obviously, growths in some areas would be impossible to find on your own, so regular dental, eye, gynecological and other exams are crucial.

But there are warning signs for some rarer melanomas. A growing brown or black streak beneath a nail should be seen by a doctor. Thumbs and big toes are most often affected. These are among the most common skin cancers in dark-skinned people. Persistent nosebleeds or a pigmented spot inside the mouth needs to be checked, too.

The good news is that most skin cancers, including most melanomas, can be found through regular self-exams and exams by doctors. Melanomas found early can be cured most of the time.

—Kim Painter

IS IT MELANOMA?

A change in a mole can signal melanoma. Or a melanoma can begin with a new growth that looks like an irregular mole. Melanomas can appear in many places on the body. They appear most often on the back and chest in men and most often on the legs in women. The neck and face are other common sites. Rarely, melanoma occurs in the eyes, inside the mouth, or in the lining of the intestinal tract.

Although people with darker skins have fewer melanomas than lighter-skinned people, they can and do get melanoma. Melanomas tend to appear on the palms of the hands, soles of the feet, and under the nails of people of color. When melanomas occur under the nails, it is usually on the thumbs and big toes. This can be mistaken for a fungal infection and may remain undetected for a long time. This delay means that people with melanoma in these locations may have a more advanced disease by the time a doctor makes the diagnosis.

Dermatologists recommend using the ABCD rule to check out moles and birthmarks. Anyone who notices even one of these signs should see a doctor right away. A doctor should also look at any spot that oozes, bleeds, itches, or crusts over.

Know Your ABCs

The ABCD rule helps you tell the difference between a normal mole and an abnormal mole or melanoma. A doctor should check a mole that has even one of the following traits.

A   Asymmetry. One half of the mole does not match the other. If the mole were folded in half, the sides would not match.

B   Border irregular. The edges of the mole are irregular, ragged, or blurred. The mole may look like a fried egg.

C   Color varies. The mole's color is not the same all over. There may be different shades of tan, brown, or black. There may be patches of pink, red, blue, or white.

D   Diameter. The mole is bigger than 0.25 inches (6 mm or the size of a pencil eraser).

E   Evolving. Some rules add E, for a mole that evolves or changes over time. A doctor should examine any mole that changes.

Often the first sign of a melanoma is a change in the size, the shape, the color, or the feel of an existing mole. Or perhaps an "ugly" new mole suddenly appears and quickly grows or changes. Most—but not all—melanomas have a blue or blue-black area. Many will feel bumpy and irregular, rather than smooth. Most fail the ABCD test.

MAKING THE DIAGNOSIS

When a person goes to a doctor with a worrisome spot, the doctor starts by taking a history and doing a physical examination. He may begin with something as simple as a bright light and a magnifying glass. Often, a better technique is needed to see if the mole might be a melanoma. The doctor might apply oil to the spot and view it with a special microscope that lets him see through the skin's surface into the next few layers.

If the doctor suspects the spot is a melanoma, he will likely remove the entire growth at once. He will numb the skin with an anesthetic and cut out the melanoma, along with an area of surrounding normal skin. That is the best way to be sure that the whole tumor is removed. Some of the types of biopsies used for basal cell and squamous cell carcinomas are not appropriate for a melanoma. For example, a shave biopsy does not show how deep into the skin a melanoma may have grown. It is seldom used to treat or diagnose melanoma.

The doctor sends the excised tissue to a pathologist for examination. If the pathologist concludes that the growth is melanoma, the dermatologist refers the patient to an oncologist, a doctor who specializes in cancer treatment, or to a surgeon for staging and treatment. The first step in staging will be to examine the lymph nodes.

For example, a man has a suspicious-looking mole on his left arm. His dermatologist removes it. The pathologist reports that the mole is actually a melanoma. The man next sees a surgeon or an oncologist. The oncologist assigns a stage to the cancer and then plans treatment. The first thing the doctor does is to examine the lymph nodes in the man's left armpit. If the cancer has spread beyond the original site on the man's arm, cancer cells will be in the lymph nodes. The doctor takes a biopsy from the lymph nodes to see if they hold any melanoma cells. The doctor may perform a needle biopsy to withdraw a small amount of cells and fluid from the lymph node.

It's easy to perform a biopsy if one of the nodes is swollen. It's trickier if the oncologist (doctor who studies cancer) cannot feel one particularly swollen lymph node. There may be dozens of lymph nodes in the region. An amazing technique called a sentinel lymph node biopsy helps pinpoint the correct node. The oncologist injects a small amount of radioactive blue dye into the area where the melanoma is located. The dye makes its way into the lymphatic system and into one specific lymph node. All lymphatic vessels in a given area drain to one primary lymph node and then on to others that are nearby.

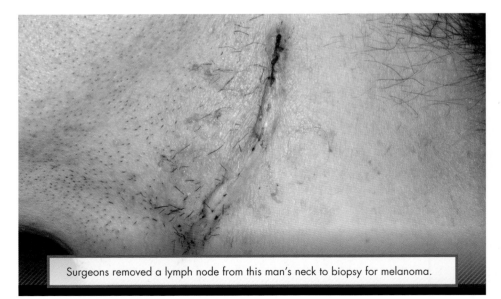

Surgeons removed a lymph node from this man's neck to biopsy for melanoma.

The doctor locates the radioactive area with a radioactivity detector. The "hot" nodes will be clumped together in the armpit. These are the nodes closest to the site of the melanoma. The doctor next cuts into the area of radiation. She removes the sentinel node, the bluest node that received the most dye. This is the node that would have cancer cells in it, if any are present. If the sentinel node does not have melanoma cells in it, no further treatment is necessary. The cancer has not metastasized.

If melanoma cells are in the sentinel node, that means the cancer has spread beyond the man's arm. The surgeon removes all the nodes in the area. Then the patient will need additional tests so that the doctor can stage the cancer. These may include chest X-rays, bone scans, and special scans called CT (computerized tomography) and MRI (magnetic resonance imaging). These tests show whether the melanoma has spread or metastasized to other parts of the man's body, such as the lungs, the bones, or the brain.

TREATMENT FOR MELANOMA

The oncologist reviews the pathology reports from the melanoma and the lymph nodes. The doctor examines the results of the various X-rays and scans. These tests usually allow the oncologist to identify the stage. Once the oncologist knows the stage, the doctor meets with the patient and his family. During the meeting, the doctor and patient discuss possible treatments, side effects, and the prognosis— the likely outcome of treatment. Patients often see another doctor for a second opinion before beginning treatment. Many experts believe that specialized cancer centers provide the best cancer care and treatment.

The earlier a melanoma is found and treated, the greater the chance of the patient recovering. When a patient knows the stage

Stages of Melanoma

Stage	Description
0	The melanoma is only in the outer layer of skin cells and has not invaded deeper tissues.
I	The melanoma is no more than 0.04 inch (1 millimeter) thick; the outer layer of skin may appear scraped or ulcerated (having sores); or, the tumor is between 0.04 and 0.08 inches (1 and 2 mm) thick with no ulceration.
II	The melanoma is between 0.04 and 0.08 inches (1 and 2 mm) thick and ulcerated, or it is thicker than 0.08 inches (2 mm) and may or may not be ulcerated.
III	The melanoma has spread to one or more nearby lymph nodes, or it has spread to tissues just outside the original tumor but not to any lymph nodes.
IV	The melanoma has spread to other organs, to lymph nodes, or to skin areas far away from the original tumor.

Source: National Cancer Institute

of the melanoma before starting treatment, it allows the patient to have an idea of what may happen in the future. The percentage of people who live for five years after being diagnosed with cancer is called the five-year survival rate. This is a general outcome averaged over many people. Any one person may have a better or worse outcome. The survival rate depends on factors such as the thickness of the melanoma, whether or not it has spread to the lymph nodes, and whether or not the patient responds to treatment. According to the American Cancer Society, the average five-year survival rate for people with melanoma is:

- Stage 0   100 percent
- Stage I   97 to 92 percent
- Stage II   81 to 53 percent
- Stage III   78 to 40 percent
- Stage IV   20 to 15 percent

Treatments for melanoma include surgery, chemotherapy, biological therapy, and radiation therapy. One treatment may be used alone, or two or more may be used together. The exact treatment depends on factors such as the melanoma's depth and whether or not it has spread to nearby tissues or distant organs.

SURGICAL TREATMENT

Surgery is the main treatment for most early-stage melanomas. Many times, surgery alone is enough to cure patients who are at stage 0 or I. If the tumor was not completely removed during the initial biopsy, the surgeon operates again. Depending on the size of the tumor, the surgeon will cut out a wide area around it to be sure of getting all the cancer cells. A skin graft from another part of the body may be needed to cover the surgical site. If the melanoma is at an early stage, Mohs surgery may be used to lessen scarring.

If the nearby lymph nodes have not already been removed, the surgeon will remove them if a biopsy showed cancer cells. Surgery may be used in more advanced stages of melanoma but usually in combination with another treatment. For example, if the melanoma has spread to the brain or lungs, surgeons may remove the tumor to make the patient more comfortable. This can also prolong the patient's life. However, if there is a metastatic tumor big enough to see on an X-ray or scan, there are probably more that are too small to see. Surgery alone is not likely to cure a person with advanced melanoma. Ultimately, most people with advanced melanoma will not survive.

CHEMOTHERAPY

Chemotherapy is the use of strong drugs to kill cancer cells. Chemotherapy does not work as well against melanoma as it does for other cancers. But doctors may use it for advanced melanoma to relieve symptoms such as pressure, pain, and, if the melanoma has spread to the brain, confusion or seizures. This makes the patient more comfortable and may extend survival. The drugs work by attacking cells that are dividing quickly. Because cancer cells are fast-growing, chemotherapy drugs work best against them.

But other cells in the body are fast-growing as well, especially bone marrow, the lining of the mouth and the intestines, and hair follicles. The chemotherapy drugs attack and damage these cells along with the cancer cells. This causes the common side effects of chemotherapy that many people experience. These include nausea and vomiting, mouth sores, loss of appetite, a decreased resistance to infection, easy bleeding, and hair loss.

Patients receive chemotherapy for a certain number of days followed by a recovery period. Then they receive more chemotherapy, followed by another recovery period. The cycle may go on for several months. Depending on the medication, patients may receive the drug by mouth or injected into a vein. Either way, the drugs enter the bloodstream and travel throughout the entire body. Nurses with special training often give injectable drugs in an outpatient clinic or in the oncologist's office.

If the melanoma is confined to an arm or a leg, doctors can give chemotherapy in a special way. During a minor surgery, doctors stop the flow of blood to and from the limb for a short time. They inject the chemotherapy drug directly into the artery that feeds the arm or the leg. This keeps most of the drug in the limb. More of it reaches the tumor and less goes into the rest of the body. Sometimes the drugs are heated before injection. This kills more cancer cells than if the drug were not heated.

Patients may receive chemotherapy in combinations of two or three different drugs to treat melanoma. Sometimes chemotherapy is combined with one of the immunotherapy drugs described later in this section.

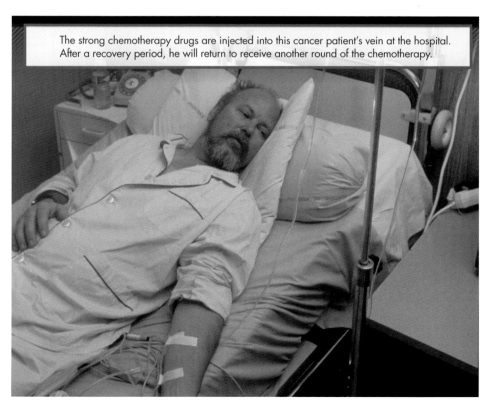

The strong chemotherapy drugs are injected into this cancer patient's vein at the hospital. After a recovery period, he will return to receive another round of the chemotherapy.

Imiquimod, the chemotherapy in cream form used for non-melanoma skin cancers, may be used for stage 0 melanomas. It is most often used on the face to prevent the scarring caused by surgery. It is applied once a day or several times a week for about three months. Imiquimod cannot be used for higher stage melanomas, and some doctors believe it shouldn't be used for melanoma at all. Surgery may be a safer option to ensure that the entire melanoma is removed.

RADIATION THERAPY

Radiation therapy uses high-energy rays to kill cancer cells. It is a common treatment for many kinds of cancer. Radiation therapy works by damaging the DNA of cancer cells so they cannot grow or divide. Radiation damages normal cells as well, but they usually

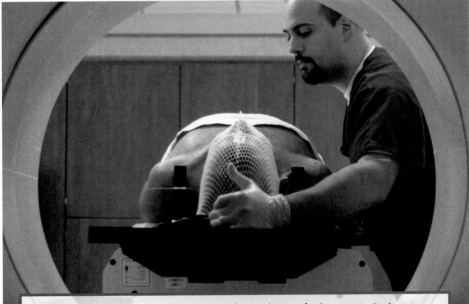

This cancer patient is about to receive radiation therapy for his cancer. Radiation damages the DNA of the cancer cells. This therapy is most often used on melanoma that has metastasized.

recover. The goal of radiation therapy is to kill as many cancer cells as possible while limiting harm to nearby healthy tissue. Radiation can be directed so it reaches only a very small area, for example, about 1 inch (2.5 cm) across. This helps keep the radiation from damaging nearby tissues and organs. Radiation therapy may be used after surgery in the area where lymph nodes were removed. This helps to kill any remaining cancer cells.

Radiation therapy is most often used to treat melanoma that has metastasized to other parts of the body. If the melanoma has traveled to the brain or the bone, radiation therapy may be used to shrink the tumor. If melanoma reaches the brain, the tumor may cause seizures or confusion. If it reaches the bone, it can cause severe pain. When radiation therapy is able to shrink the tumor, it may make patients more comfortable by controlling their symptoms.

IMMUNOTHERAPY

While chemotherapy directly attacks cancer cells, immunotherapy helps the immune system to fight cancer. The immune system includes the spleen, the lymph nodes, bone marrow, tonsils, and several types of white blood cells. It works hard to fight off cancer (as well as bacterial and viral infections). Immunotherapy stimulates a patient's own immune system to recognize and fight cancer cells. It is one of the newest advances in cancer treatment. Immunotherapy does three things to stop the progress of cancer:

1. It stops or slows the growth of cancer cells.
2. It makes it easier for the immune system to destroy cancer cells.
3. It keeps cancer from spreading to other parts of the body.

The immunotherapy medications used to treat melanoma are called cytokines. Cytokines are proteins that the body normally makes in small amounts. They naturally stimulate the immune system to fight infections and other diseases. But the body cannot make enough cytokines to fight off cancer. Scientists have been able to manufacture synthetic versions of cytokines in the large amounts needed for that job. Immunotherapy is generally used for patients with stages III and IV melanoma. When used alone, the medications are effective in about 10 to 20 percent of people. In some patients with later-stage melanomas, immunotherapy is given after surgery or with chemotherapy.

The two types of cytokines used to treat melanoma are interferon-alpha and interleukin-2. Some patients must be hospitalized in order to receive the high doses of interleukin needed to treat melanoma. Interferon may be injected at a clinic or a doctor's office. In some cases, the patient or a family member can inject it at home. Side effects of cytokines include fever, chills, aches, depression, and severe fatigue. Some patients must stop the medications because of these side effects. Others can complete the treatment without major problems.

Melanoma is aggressive and fast-growing. Once it has spread to the lymph nodes or to distant sites, melanoma is very hard to treat. It is resistant to forms of treatment that are successful with other cancers. The long-term outcome for stage IV melanoma is often grim. But many scientists at cancer hospitals and research laboratories are looking for better ways to find and treat melanoma.

The surgery to remove the melanoma on Nate's back took three and a half hours. The doctor removed the melanoma, a big area of surrounding tissue, and three nearby lymph nodes. Tests showed the cancer had reached one of the lymph nodes. "I was scared. It was serious. It shocked me," Nate said. He had twenty interferon treatments to help his body fight off the cancer. The interferon gave Nate cold sweats and severe headaches.

After Nate finished the treatment, doctors removed a smaller melanoma on his abdomen. Now when Nate takes off his shirt at the pool or the beach, he uses sunscreen. He smears it over the 2-inch (5 cm) scar on his stomach. He smears it over the 6-inch (15 cm) scar on his back. "I'm twenty-three years old now, still young," he says. "I have a long way to go. I want to grow old. The fact is, I could have died."

CHAPTER FIVE

PREVENTING SKIN CANCER

Brian Halvorson is a physical education teacher in North Dakota. During high school and college, he worked as a lifeguard without using sunscreen. "I never really thought about protecting myself from sun exposure," he said. A few years ago, he noticed a red dot on one cheek but thought it was a pimple. He didn't see a doctor about it for six months. When he did finally go to the doctor, a biopsy showed that Brian had melanoma. Two weeks later, the doctor cut out the spot. Two months later, the doctor discovered a swollen lymph node in his neck. Tests showed the cancer had spread.

Lifeguards, who spend hours in the hot sun, need to be sure to protect themselves with a strong sunscreen to prevent skin cancers later in life.

Brian went for treatment at a cancer center where doctors found more cancer in his neck. They worried it had spread to his spine. Four out of five people who get melanoma in the spine die in less than five years. "They did an MRI on my spine. I went twenty-four hours thinking I wasn't going to live," Brian said. Even though the MRI showed the melanoma had not reached the spine, Brian needed more surgery and radiation to his neck. "The doctors told me that all my damage was done when I was a lifeguard and never protected myself. I teach kids. I need to tell them about prevention."

Skin cancer is the most preventable kind of cancer. Even so, more than one million Americans develop it each year. Most of these people failed to do enough to protect themselves from the sun's ultraviolet radiation. Others spent too much time in tanning salons seeking the perfect "sun-kissed" look. And a few people were unfortunate enough to be born with genes that increased their risk of developing skin cancer. Yet it is easy to do the right things to greatly reduce the chance of getting skin cancer.

LIMIT SUN EXPOSURE

The dangers of ultraviolet radiation are well known. It's the primary cause of skin cancer, and it leads to premature aging of the skin. It makes good sense to protect yourself from getting too much sun. For example, stay in the shade between ten in the morning and four in the afternoon. Those are the hours the sun's rays are strongest. One way to estimate how much UV exposure you are getting is to look at your shadow. If your shadow is taller than you are (in the early morning and late afternoon), your UV exposure is fairly low. If your shadow is shorter than you are (during the middle of the day), you are being exposed to high levels of UV radiation.

Scientists developed the ultraviolet index to measure the sun's UV radiation. It is used around the world to tell people about the risk of UV radiation on a given day. The Environmental Protection Agency (www.epa.gov/sunwise/uvindex.html) maps the UV Index across the nation each day. You can look up your state to get an idea of how dangerous the sun will be on any given day.

The numbers and suggested activities for each of the levels are:

2 or less   Low risk. Danger from the sun's UV rays is low for the average person. Wear sunglasses on bright days. If you burn easily, cover up and use sunscreen.

3–5   Moderate risk. There is a moderate risk of harm from unprotected sun exposure. Take precautions, such as covering up if you will be outside. Stay in the shade during the middle of the day when the sun is strongest.

6–7   High risk. There is a high risk of harm from unprotected sun exposure. Use sunscreen, wear a wide-brimmed hat and sunglasses. Limit time spent in the sun between ten A.M. and four P.M.

8–10   Very high risk. There is a very high risk of harm from unprotected sun exposure. Stay out of the sun between ten in the morning and four in the afternoon if possible. Use sunscreen liberally, wear protective clothing, and put on sunglasses. Seek out shade. Unprotected skin will burn quickly.

11+   Extreme risk. There is an extreme risk of skin damage from unprotected sun exposure. Apply sunscreen liberally every two hours while outside. Better yet, stay inside. Seek shade and cover up. Wear long-sleeved clothing, a wide-brimmed hat, and sunglasses. Unprotected skin can burn in minutes.

This warning sign in Nevada lights up to show the amount of protection visitors need depending on the strength of the sun.

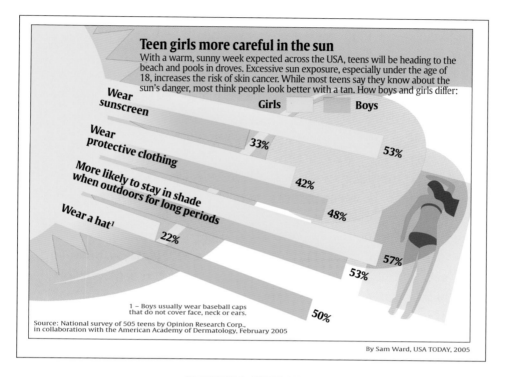

Teen girls more careful in the sun

With a warm, sunny week expected across the USA, teens will be heading to the beach and pools in droves. Excessive sun exposure, especially under the age of 18, increases the risk of skin cancer. While most teens say they know about the sun's danger, most think people look better with a tan. How boys and girls differ:

	Girls	Boys
Wear sunscreen	33%	53%
Wear protective clothing	42%	
More likely to stay in shade when outdoors for long periods	48%	57%
Wear a hat[1]	22%	53%
	50%	

1 – Boys usually wear baseball caps that do not cover face, neck or ears.

Source: National survey of 505 teens by Opinion Research Corp., in collaboration with the American Academy of Dermatology, February 2005

By Sam Ward, USA TODAY, 2005

TREATING SUNBURN

You should do everything you can to avoid getting sunburned. But if you do, here are some things you should know. Not only is a sunburn painful, it is dangerous and tells you that the sun has damaged your skin. It can take twenty-four hours before the full extent of a sunburn is visible. Sunburns are actually first-degree and second-degree burns.

A first-degree sunburn causes redness. It will heal, usually with some peeling, within a few days. The American Academy of Dermatology (AAD) says to use cool baths, moisturizers, and over-the-counter (OTC) hydrocortisone creams to relieve the dry, painful skin of a first-degree sunburn. OTC pain medications such as acetaminophen (the ingredient in Tylenol) and ibuprofen (the ingredient in Advil and Motrin) may help the pain. (Teens and children should never use aspirin or any product containing aspirin without a doctor's approval. Aspirin can lead to the rare but potentially deadly condition called Reye's syndrome in young people.) The AAD also says not to use OTC anesthetic (numbing) ointments such as benzocaine. They can cause allergic reactions in some people.

A second-degree sunburn causes blisters. This is a sign of damage to the deeper layers of skin. Anyone who gets a headache, fever, or chills with a second-degree sunburn should seek medical help immediately. People can take care of a small area of second-degree sunburn at home. They may take an OTC medication for pain but should not apply any type of cream or moisturizer to the blistered area unless a doctor advises them to do so. Never break blisters. They help to protect damaged skin, and breaking blisters delays healing. It may also allow the damaged skin to become infected. Layers of gauze can be used to cover the burned skin until it heals.

SLIP, SLOP, AND SLAP

It's nearly impossible to avoid sun exposure entirely, and most of us would not wish to do so. Whether it's a trip to the beach with friends, outdoor sports, or time in the park, many of our favorite activities involve being outside. The good news is that there are several things you can do to protect your skin from sunlight's UV radiation. Easy to remember and easy to do, these actions make it safer to spend time in the sun. So slip, slop, slap . . . and wrap so that you can enjoy a little sunshine.

SLIP ON A SHIRT

Wear clothing to protect as much of your skin as possible from the sun. Clothing provides different levels of protection from UV radiation.

www.usatoday.com

Life
SECTION D

June 4, 2007

From the Pages of USA TODAY

Suit up and stop the sun
Treated clothing provides additional line of defense

Can your clothes protect your health? The UPF [ultraviolet protection factor] ratings you increasingly see on clothes tags are comparable to the SPF (sun protection factor) ratings you see on sunscreens and cosmetics. In other words, if your arm is covered by a fabric with a UPF rating of 30, it will take that arm 30 times longer to become sunburned than if you went sleeveless.

Clothing manufacturers obtain the ratings from testing labs that use a device called a spectrophotometer to measure the passage of ultraviolet light through fabrics (some of which have been treated with chemicals to enhance their protective qualities). The testing is "quite well established and standardized," and the resulting ratings are "a good indication of how protective the clothing is," says Henry Lim, chairman of the department of dermatology at Henry Ford Hospital in Detroit.

The ratings should be considered reliable, says Kathryn Hatch, a textile scientist at the University of Arizona–Tucson. Hatch says consumers at high risk for sun damage—for example, those with pale skin,

outdoor jobs, heightened sun sensitivity or previous skin cancers—also might consider a wash-in sun-protection booster on cotton, linen and rayon garments.

—Kim Painter

This child playing on the beach is wearing a swimsuit with UV protection and a hat with a large brim.

Long-sleeved shirts, long pants, and long skirts offer the most protection. Tightly woven fabrics (such as thick cotton) are better than thinner fabrics such as a T-shirt. If you can see light through the fabric, it offers little protection. Dry fabric provides more protection than wet. Remember that UV radiation can penetrate light clothing.

Some sports clothing is made so that it protects against UV exposure, even when wet. These clothes have a label stating the ultraviolet protection factor (UPF). The UPF ranges from 15 to 50. The higher the number, the more protection the clothing offers against UV radiation. The fabrics are lightweight and comfortable. Increasingly, sun-protective fabrics are used to make children's swimwear.

Products are available to increase the UPF value of regular clothing. They are added to the laundry just like a detergent is. The products add temporary UV protection to your clothes without changing the color or texture of the fabric.

Slip, Slop, Slap! . . . and Wrap

To help protect yourself from skin cancer:

- Slip on a shirt (long-sleeved is best).
- Slop on the sunscreen (at least SPF 15).
- Slap on a hat (wide-brimmed to protect neck and ears).
- Wrap on sunglasses to protect the eyes.

SLOP ON THE SUNSCREEN

A poll by *Consumer Reports* found that one-third of Americans never use sunscreen. The poll showed that more than one-fourth of people never or rarely use it on their children, even if they are in the sun for several hours! Respondents said they didn't use sunscreen because it gets in their eyes and makes sand stick to their skin. Other people worried about the cost of sunscreen or were bothered by the smell. Some didn't like to feel the sunscreen on their hands. Sunscreen helps to protect the skin from damaging UV radiation. People who don't use sunscreen risk getting skin cancer.

The first thing to know about sunscreen is the SPF. The sun protection factor is the number displayed on the product label, and it ranges from 8 to 80. The number measures the product's ability to screen the sun's harmful rays. According to the American Melanoma Foundation, SPF 15 means that you can be in the sun fifteen times longer than you can without sunscreen before burning. For example, a fair-skinned woman may burn in the sun after ten minutes without sunscreen. If she wears a sunscreen with an SPF of 15, she probably would not burn for 150 minutes. Even so, sunscreen should be reapplied every two hours (120 minutes) for best results.

The UV protection does not increase proportionally with an increased SPF number. An SPF of 15 screens out about

This red-haired, light-skinned woman is making sure to cover her skin with a high SPF sunscreen.

93 percent of UV rays. A sunscreen with an SPF of 30 screens out about 97 percent of the UV rays. Dermatologists recommend that everyone use a sunscreen with an SPF of 15 or more all year. People with fair skin or those who burn easily should use one with a higher SPF. Because UVA rays can go through glass, doctors say to wear sunscreen all the time, not just when you'll be outside.

Sunscreens come in many forms: creams, lotions, gels, oils, sprays, and ointments. Follow these tips when choosing and using a sunscreen:

- Choose a broad-spectrum sunscreen that protects against both UVA and UVB. A chemical called PABA (para-aminobenzoic acid) helps to protect against UVB, though some people seem to be allergic to PABA. Sunscreens that contain oxybenzone, sulisbobenzone, and avobenzone protect against UVA. Creams with titanium dioxide and zinc oxide are very effective at blocking both UVA and UVB rays. These are the thick white creams you often see smeared down someone's nose.

- Apply sunscreen properly. For best results, apply it to dry skin twenty to thirty minutes before going outside. This gives your skin time to absorb the sunscreen.

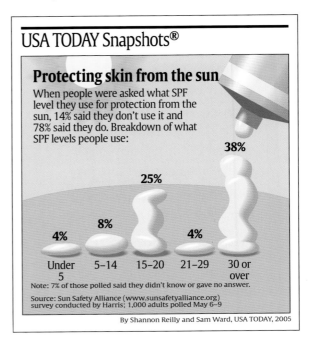

USA TODAY Snapshots®

Protecting skin from the sun

When people were asked what SPF level they use for protection from the sun, 14% said they don't use it and 78% said they do. Breakdown of what SPF levels people use:

- Under 5: 4%
- 5–14: 8%
- 15–20: 25%
- 21–29: 4%
- 30 or over: 38%

Note: 7% of those polled said they didn't know or gave no answer.

Source: Sun Safety Alliance (www.sunsafetyalliance.org) survey conducted by Harris; 1,000 adults polled May 6–9

By Shannon Reilly and Sam Ward, USA TODAY, 2005

June 1, 2009

From the Pages of USA TODAY

Sunscreen isn't just about SPF

When you read a sunscreen label, don't skip the fine print. Consumers who want to save their skin need to be vigilant, sun protection experts say, because confusing, sometimes misleading labels line drugstore shelves.

"There's a misconception that the SPF number is all you need to know," says Sonya Lunder, a senior analyst for the Environmental Working Group, a non-profit watchdog group that studies sunscreen ingredients and labels.

Here are other things savvy label readers should know:

- The truth about SPF. These numbers reflect how well a product screens out ultraviolet B (UVB) rays, which cause burning and contribute to skin cancer. An SPF of 15 means unprotected skin would burn 15 times faster than skin slathered with a thick coating of the product.
- The skinny on UVA. Labels don't have to say anything about how well a product screens ultraviolet A (UVA) rays, which penetrate deeper than UVB rays and contribute to skin aging and cancer. Under proposed FDA rules, UVA protection will be rated on a four-star scale. For now, consumers should look for labels that tout "broad spectrum" protection and list ingredients known to screen UVA rays, says dermatologist David Pariser of Norfolk, Va., president of the American Academy of Dermatology.
- The key ingredients. Look for avobenzone, oxybenzone, titanium dioxide, zinc oxide or ecamsule. An effective broad-spectrum sunscreen should contain one or more of those, says the Skin Cancer Foundation.
- Two terms to take with a grain of salt. "Waterproof" (there's no such thing because all sunscreens wash, rub or sweat off) and "sunblock" (these products screen but do not block the sun's rays), says Henry Lim, chairman of the department of dermatology at Henry Ford Hospital in Dearborn, Mich., and a spokesman for the Skin Cancer Foundation.

Everyone who uses sunscreen should also limit time in the sun and wear protective clothing when possible. Under the proposed new rules, all sunscreen labels will say all three steps are important. In other words, sunscreen is no substitute for common sense, hats, sunglasses, sleeves and shade.

—*Kim Painter*

- Use enough sunscreen. Most people use only one-third to one-half of the amount they should use. Use about 1 ounce (28 grams) with each application. That's enough to fill the palm of your cupped hand. Reapply sunscreen every two hours if you are swimming, sweating, or drying yourself off with a towel. A water-resistant sunscreen maintains its full SPF level for only forty minutes in water. A waterproof sunscreen lasts eighty minutes in water.
- Apply sunscreen to all exposed skin. Pay special attention to the face, the ears, the hands, the tops of feet, and the arms. Lips are especially sensitive. Use a lip balm that contains sunscreen with an SPF of 15 or more.
- The American Academy of Dermatology gives a Seal of Recognition to help people choose the best sunscreens. (Go to www.aad.org, and search for the Seal of Recognition to find dermatologist-recommended sunscreens.)
- Sunscreens expire in two to three years. Check the expiration date.

Text Message: Put on Sunscreen

A report published in the medical journal *Archives of Dermatology* in 2009 found that people who received a daily text message to use sunscreen applied it nearly twice as often as those who received no text message or a text message about another subject. Researchers fitted tubes of sunscreen with electronic monitors that told them when people opened their sunscreen. Study participants said they would continue to apply sunscreen on a daily basis and would tell their friends to do it as well.

SLAP ON A HAT

Skin cancer is common on the neck, the ears, the forehead, the nose, and the scalp, areas often exposed to the sun. Wear a hat with a brim at least 2 to 3 inches (5 to 8 cm) wide for best protection against the sun. An even better choice is a shade cap, which looks like a baseball cap with fabric hanging down the sides and the back. These caps are sold in sports and camping stores.

Straw hats are not recommended for sun protection because they are too loosely woven. UV radiation can still reach the head and the face. Baseball caps do a good job of protecting the forehead and top of the head, but not the neck or the ears.

WRAP ON SUNGLASSES

Spending long hours in the sun increases the risk of certain eye diseases, such as melanoma and cataracts. While rare, melanoma of the eye does occur. Basal cell and squamous cell carcinomas are common on the eyelids and the delicate skin around the eyes. Wearing UV-blocking sunglasses can help protect your eyes from sun damage. Children should have smaller versions of real sunglasses, not toy plastic ones.

Sunglasses don't have to be expensive to protect your eyes. But they should block 99 to 100 percent of both UVA and UVB radiation. The label will tell you how much radiation the sunglasses block. Sunglasses marked "cosmetic" block about 70 percent of UV rays. If the label does not say anything about UV protection, the sunglasses likely offer little or no protection.

Sunglasses with large frames or those that wrap around your face keep sunlight from coming in around the edges. Darker glasses may be more comfortable in bright sunlight, but they don't necessarily offer greater protection. UV protection comes from an invisible coating applied to the lenses. It doesn't matter how dark the glasses are or what color the lenses are. What matters is how much UV protection they provide.

People who wear prescription eyeglasses should change to prescription sunglasses when they are in the sun. They can also use clip-on sunglasses with UV protection over their regular glasses. If you wear contact lenses, ask your eye doctor if they block UV radiation. Some do. However, contact lenses don't protect the rest of the eye area, and good sunglasses are still the best option.

TANNING BEDS — AS DANGEROUS AS PLUTONIUM!

Have you ever relaxed in a tanning bed? Think twice before doing it again. In June 2009, the World Health Organization's (WHO's) International Agency for Research on Cancer (IARC) announced that the ultraviolet radiation put out by tanning beds causes cancer. WHO moved tanning beds into the highest cancer risk category, naming them as carcinogenic (cancer causing) to humans. Also in the highest cancer risk category are arsenic, asbestos, cigarettes, mustard gas, plutonium, and radon gas. Ultraviolet radiation, whether it comes from the sun or from tanning beds, is a big risk factor for all forms of skin cancer.

Tanning beds (sometimes called sunbeds) are used most often in affluent countries in the Northern Hemisphere, especially the United States and Europe. An analysis of twenty studies from those countries showed that people who use tanning beds before the age of thirty have a 75 percent increase in their risk for melanoma. Melanoma of the eye is also associated with tanning beds. Dr. Vincent Cogliano, a member of the IARC, said, "People mistakenly see a tan as a sign of health when it is actually a sign of damage to the skin."

Governments of several countries are taking steps to protect young people from the cancer risk associated with tanning beds.

Germany passed a law banning people younger than eighteen years old from going to tanning salons, or solariums as they are known in some countries. England, Scotland, Ireland, and Wales are likely to do the same. "We hope the prevailing culture will change so teens don't think they need to use sunbeds to get a tan," Dr. Cogliano said.

In the United States, nearly two dozen states and dozens of counties are working on laws to limit tanning salon use by children and teens. For example, a law proposed in Texas would require a doctor's note, a parent's written consent, and a parent in attendance for anyone younger than eighteen to use a tanning bed. Ohio would require a doctor's prescription as well. Arkansas, Illinois, Maryland, Mississippi, New Jersey, and New York already have laws or are proposing laws to prevent children and teens from using tanning salons.

There are safe and effective ways to achieve the tanned look. The U. S. Food and Drug Administration (FDA) has approved certain "bronzers" for cosmetic use. Bronzers are color additives that temporarily stain the skin to mimic a tan. They are easily removed with soap and water. The FDA has also approved the color additive dihydroxyacetone, or DHA, for use in sunless tanners. These lotions, creams, and sprays combine with protein on the skin's surface to produce color. The tan color lasts for several days.

Some tanning salons offer whole body sprays in tanning booths. The best artificial tans last for ten days to two weeks. While these products leave people with a tanned look, they offer no protection against the damaging effects of UV radiation. People who use sunless tanners should remove them before spending time in the sun. Then they need to apply sunscreen.

Beware of other so-called tanning products that have not been approved by the FDA. Some tanning pills contain the chemical that makes carrots orange. Taken in large quantities, the pills can turn the skin an orange tan color. However, they can also seriously damage the eyes and the liver. Tanning accelerators are another type of product not approved by the FDA. Companies may market these as products that stimulate the body's own tanning process. The FDA considers tanning pills and tanning accelerators as unproven and potentially dangerous.

MAP YOUR MOLES

Doctors may recommend that certain people routinely examine their skin for possible skin cancer. This could include people who have had skin cancer or those who are at high risk for it. The AAD developed the Body Mole Map for this purpose. The map lets people note their moles, where they are, and how or if they change. This makes it simpler to track moles and other unusual marks on the body. Doing the skin self-exam on the same day each month makes it easier to remember.

The most convenient time to do a skin self-exam is after a shower or bath. For best results, use a full-length mirror and a large handheld mirror in a room with good lighting. The first month, you can start out by learning where your birthmarks, moles, and blemishes are. You want to know what they look like and how they feel to the touch. You can chart existing spots on the Body Mole Map. The second month, check for new moles or marks that look unusual; a change in the size, the shape, the color, or the texture of an existing mole; or a sore that does not heal.

Check yourself from head to toe. Remember to check all areas of your skin, including your back, your scalp, between the buttocks, and the genital area. Follow these steps to be sure you cover all areas:

- Stand in front of the full-length mirror and look at your face, neck, ears, chest, and belly.
- Raise your arms, and look at your left and right sides and your armpits.

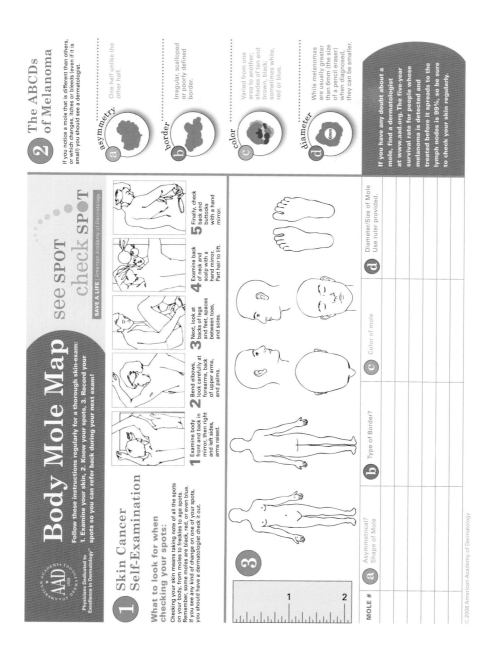

Body Mole Map

see SPOT
check SPOT

SAVE A LIFE | American Academy of Dermatology

Physicians Dedicated to Excellence in Dermatology®

Follow these instructions regularly for a thorough skin-exam: 1. Examine your skin, 2. Know your spots, 3. Record your spots so you can refer back during your next exam!

1 Skin Cancer Self-Examination

What to look for when checking your spots:

Checking your skin means taking note of all the spots on your body, from moles to freckles to age spots. Remember, some moles are black, red, or even blue. If you see any kind of change on one of your spots, you should have a dermatologist check it out.

1 Examine body front and back in mirror, then right and left sides, arms raised.

2 Bend elbows, look carefully at forearms, back of upper arms, and palms.

3 Next, look at backs of legs and feet, spaces between toes, and soles.

4 Examine back of neck and scalp with a hand mirror. Part hair to lift.

5 Finally, check back and buttocks with a hand mirror.

2 The ABCDs of Melanoma

If you notice a mole that is different than others, or which changes, itches or bleeds (even if it is small) you should see a dermatologist.

asymmetry
(a) One half unlike the other half.

border
(b) Irregular, scalloped or poorly defined border.

color
(c) Varied from one area to another; shades of tan and brown, black; sometimes white, red or blue.

diameter
(d) While melanomas are usually greater than 6mm (the size of a pencil eraser) when diagnosed, they can be smaller.

If you have any doubt about a mole, find a dermatologist at www.aad.org. The five-year survival rate for people whose melanoma is detected and treated before it spreads to the lymph nodes is 99%, so be sure to check your skin regularly.

3

MOLE #	(a) Asymmetrical? Shape of Mole	(b) Type of Border?	(c) Color of mole	(d) Diameter/Size of Mole Use ruler provided.

© 2008 American Academy of Dermatology

Charting moles on a Body Mole Map like this one is an important part of good skin health. Noticing changes in moles allows people to catch skin cancer early, which greatly increases survival rates.

The Vitamin D Dilemma

Vitamin D, sometimes called the sunshine vitamin, is good for the bones and the immune system, and it helps regulate blood pressure. Vitamin D also may help to prevent certain types of cancer. Yet many people do not get enough of this important vitamin.

Human skin makes vitamin D when exposed to sunlight. It takes just ten to fifteen minutes of sunlight a few days a week on unprotected skin to make enough vitamin D. People spend less time outdoors than they used to. And many people use sunscreen when they are outside. Sunscreen prevents the skin from making vitamin D.

We can get vitamin D from food and from supplements (in vitamin pills or vitamin D capsules). Vitamin D is naturally found in fish. It is added to milk and orange juice. But that may not be enough. It's difficult to get enough vitamin D from food alone. Some doctors say we should get our vitamin D from a combination of sunshine, food, and supplements.

Other doctors say it is not safe to spend any time in the sunshine without using sunscreen. The National Council on Skin Cancer Prevention says we should get all of our vitamin D from food and supplements. The American Academy of Dermatology agrees that we should not rely on sunlight exposure to unprotected skin as a source of vitamin D.

More time in the sun or more vitamin D pills? There is no one answer that's right for everyone. The vitamin D dilemma is a riddle that does not yet have a solution.

- Using the full-length and handheld mirrors, look at the front and the back of each arm and each leg.
- With the mirrors, look at your entire back and hips from the neck down.
- Examine your buttocks and genital areas.
- Look at your fingernails, the back of your hands, the palms, and the front and the back of each finger.
- Sit down and check the top and sole of each foot, between the toes, and the toenails.
- Use a comb or hairdryer set on cool to move your hair so that you can examine your scalp.

At a minimum, check your birthday suit on your birthday! Doing it more often can increase the chance of finding anything abnormal. Early discovery and treatment of skin cancer can result in a complete cure. See a doctor right away about any suspicious mole or unusual spot that worries you.

After teacher Brian Halvorson finished his cancer treatments, he began to visit high schools to talk to students about melanoma. He explained how too much exposure to the sun and tanning beds are major risk factors for melanoma. He told kids how doctors find and treat melanoma.

A senior named Jay Jelinek got a little worried. "Mr. Halvorson talked about moles and what they'd look like if they were melanoma. I had some like that on my back." Jay's mom took him to the doctor. One of his moles was an early melanoma. "The doctors removed it without having to do radiation or anything like that," he says. "I definitely use a lot more sunscreen now and avoid the sun as much as I can." Jay went on to play football for the University of North Dakota.

CHAPTER SIX

LIFE AFTER SKIN CANCER

*M*aryAnn Gerber was twenty-four when a doctor told her that the reddish mole on her face was melanoma. MaryAnn had been going to a tanning salon almost weekly for four years. "The reason I tanned so much was because I was vain about my looks," she said. The spot on her face sent her to the doctor a couple of months later. "The mole wasn't black, so it never occurred to me that it could be cancer. Also, I was young, so I didn't feel at risk." It's a good thing she didn't wait any longer.

"The doctor found another melanoma on my lower back and a basal cell carcinoma on my neck," she said. "During my first surgery, the doctor removed the melanomas and a few lymph nodes. In the second surgery, he removed every lymph node on the left side of my neck—nearly thirty of them! A third surgery removed the basal cell carcinoma." MaryAnn blames tanning beds for her cancer. "I followed the guidelines and never burned. I put a towel over my face. But twenty minutes in a tanning bed is equal to three hours in the sun."

Skin cancer often can be completely cured when it is discovered early. Still, if you've had skin cancer, it's natural to worry that it will come back or that a new one will develop. People who have had skin cancer may be concerned about needing further surgery or being left with more scars. If you've had skin cancer, you may wonder if life will ever be the same again. Will you be able to spend time outdoors with family and friends? How about going to the beach or the pool? Camping or hiking? And what about outdoor sports?

Most people need to make only small changes in their lives to reduce their risks of getting skin cancer again. Others need to adjust to living with cancer and perhaps to receiving ongoing treatment.

The frequency of follow-up visits and possible additional treatment depends on what kind of skin cancer a person had.

BASAL CELL AND SQUAMOUS CELL CARCINOMA

There is no way to undo long years of sun damage. Anyone who has had basal cell or squamous cell carcinoma has a higher risk of developing more of them than a person who never had skin cancer. If these skin cancers do return or new ones develop, it is most likely to happen within the first five years after treatment.

It is important for people to have follow-up examinations as recommended by their doctors. Some dermatologists photograph every mole or unusual spot and mark it on a special chart so that it is easy to track changes over time. During the visits, the doctor will carefully examine the skin and feel for swollen lymph nodes. He may order a CT scan or MRI for people whose cancer has spread to the lymph nodes before treatment.

For basal cell carcinomas, doctors usually advise patients to visit every six months for the first few years. If no further basal cell carcinomas develop, yearly visits should be enough. Squamous cell carcinomas can be more serious. These patients may need to see their doctors every six months for several years. After that, visits may drop to once a year.

Skin cancer patients also need follow-up medical visits to watch for possible side effects of cancer treatments. Some treatments, such as minor surgery, are unlikely to cause any problems or complications. People who have had chemotherapy, radiation, or medications that affect the immune system may have side effects for a longer period of time. However, in most cases, people will feel well in a few months.

People who have had skin cancer need to take extra steps to protect themselves from the sun. They should always use sunscreen, wear

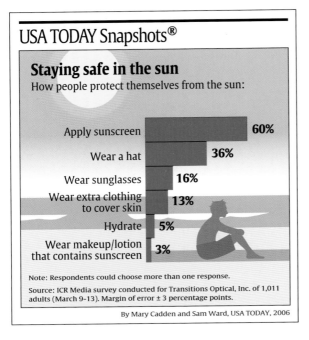

USA TODAY Snapshots®

Staying safe in the sun
How people protect themselves from the sun:

Apply sunscreen	60%
Wear a hat	36%
Wear sunglasses	16%
Wear extra clothing to cover skin	13%
Hydrate	5%
Wear makeup/lotion that contains sunscreen	3%

Note: Respondents could choose more than one response.

Source: ICR Media survey conducted for Transitions Optical, Inc. of 1,011 adults (March 9-13). Margin of error ± 3 percentage points.

By Mary Cadden and Sam Ward, USA TODAY, 2006

hats and sunglasses, and avoid midday sun. On days when the UV index is especially high, they should consider staying indoors entirely. Remember that all UV radiation penetrates clouds, and some of it penetrates glass. Light-colored surfaces such as sand and water increase its effects. Recovering from any kind of skin cancer can be a good time for people to think about the choices they made in the past. It provides the perfect opportunity to make healthier lifestyle choices for the future.

AFTER MELANOMA

Many people who have had melanoma have survived a potentially deadly disease. When caught in the very earliest stage, melanoma can be completely curable. But all too often it is discovered at a later, more advanced stage. Modern treatments allow more people with advanced melanoma to survive than in the past. That's what happened to MaryAnn, Nate, and Brian.

People who have had melanoma need to see their doctors frequently. For thin, early-stage melanomas, doctors recommend visits every three to twelve months for several years. If the exams are normal, once a year after that may be enough. For thicker or

July 9, 2008

From the Pages of USA TODAY

Sneaking in a little face time with Old Sol

Like millions of Americans, I went to the beach last week. And while a couple of the days were foggy and gray, it didn't matter. I was at the beach. I've been known to go in the rain. Maybe it's the ritual I like best. The towels, the *People* magazine, the dozens of tubes of sunscreen stuffed into a canvas bag.

We trudge over the dunes, set up our beach chairs and spend the afternoon staring out to sea, just as we have for years. Front-row seats for whatever floats by—seals, surfers, a sailboat or two. All right there before our eyes.

The one thing that has changed over the years is the sun. We have to avoid it now. A bit of a problem since the sun is as much a part of the beach as the sand and the sea.

Gone are the days of basting in baby oil, sizzling on a silver reflector blanket, baking on one side for an hour, then turning over to bake the other side until well done. Or at least medium rare.

I cheat on occasion. I still sit in the sun long enough to get "color," as we call it. But then I put on my hat and my T-shirt and pretend to be a grown-up who actually listens to what his doctor has to say.

My reward for being good? A perfect farmer's tan. My arms and neck are nice and brown. My body white. Not necessarily the look one strives for. Tan lines are not always sexy. But those are the lines I have been given. Worse fates have befallen a beachgoer. Raccoon eyes for sunglass wearers, for one.

Compared with my partner, Jack, I am a bronzed god. He spent last week sitting under a baseball cap, wrapped from head to toe in beach towels. A few melanoma scares have sent him undercover.

I suspect people walking by didn't even realize there was a human in that beach chair. Just a mound of towels topped with a hat. A mummy maybe. They scurried on, heads down, asking no questions, which is just the way it should be.

—*Craig Wilson*

more advanced melanomas, people may need to see their doctors every three to six months for two years, and then every three to twelve months for two more years. The visits typically decrease to once a year after that.

Doctors may perform follow-up imaging studies such as CT scans, chest X-rays, and blood tests more often in melanoma survivors. Melanoma may return to the same site or may appear in a distant site ten or more years after it was first treated. The risk of recurrent or metastatic melanoma is much greater than for non-melanoma skin cancers.

Melanoma survivors should check their own skin and feel for swollen lymph nodes monthly. Having had one melanoma is a risk factor for having a second or a third. People who have had melanoma are also more likely to develop non-melanoma skin cancers. Of course, people who have had melanoma should be extremely careful to protect themselves from sun damage in the future.

People with melanoma stage I and higher may have received chemotherapy, immunotherapy, or radiation. Perhaps they needed treatment for many months. These people share many of the same problems, such as nausea, fatigue, and pain, that people having treatment for any kind of cancer experience.

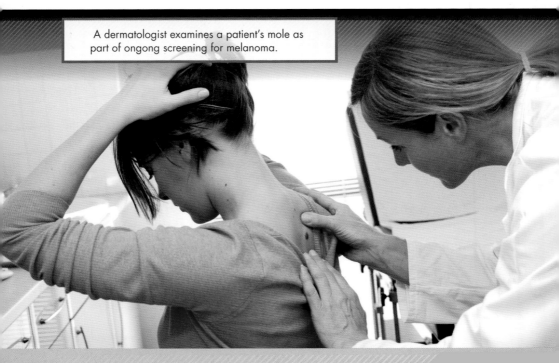

A dermatologist examines a patient's mole as part of ongong screening for melanoma.

LOSS OF APPETITE

A diet is all the food and liquids you eat and drink. It's important for everyone to follow a healthy diet and to eat the right foods. That includes eating well-balanced meals that are low in fat, sugar, and salt. Whole grain bread, cereal, and pasta, along with a wide assortment of fruits, nuts, and vegetables, make up a healthy diet.

But eating right can be a challenge for people receiving cancer treatment. People often experience nausea or loss of appetite, especially if they are on chemotherapy, or taking interferon or interleukin. Medication can make foods taste odd. Radiation can cause pain and sores in the mouth. It is common for people undergoing cancer treatment to lose weight. These problems usually resolve when the treatment is over.

People may need to change their eating habits during cancer treatment. Eating five to six small meals each day may be easier than eating three big meals a day. Eating very small amounts every couple of hours may help to decrease nausea. There are medications for cancer patients that help to control nausea. A dietitian can help people select foods that are nutritious and easy to eat.

FATIGUE

Severe fatigue may be the most common problem for people undergoing treatment for cancer, including melanoma. There are the frequent visits to doctors and clinics for treatment, the ongoing worry, the side effects of treatment, and the immune system's constant fight against the cancer. It's no surprise that fatigue goes along with cancer treatment and that it may last for a long time after treatment is over.

Doing everyday things can be difficult. People with cancer-related fatigue need to learn to manage the energy they have. Many people feel better in the morning. They have less fatigue early in the day.

Morning might be the best time to go shopping, keep medical and dental appointments, and visit friends. A person with fatigue related to cancer treatment probably will not want to visit the doctor and go grocery shopping the same morning, maybe not even the same day. Instead, it might be better to plan the week's activities to conserve energy.

For some people, fatigue comes on suddenly. They must stop what they are doing and rest. Many people learn to make time for an afternoon nap. A nap of only thirty minutes can be a big energy booster. Busy people who have never napped during the day may be surprised to discover how much better they feel when they are rested.

EXERCISE AND WEAKNESS

People might wonder why they should exercise when they already feel tired and weak. People being treated for cancer and those who are recovering should check with their doctors before starting an exercise program. Exercise generally helps people feel better and may even improve their response to cancer treatment. Most people will be able to perform some kind of exercise. Exercise can reduce anxiety and depression, increase energy and alertness, improve functioning of the heart and lungs, strengthen muscles, and improve your well-being and self-image.

It is not necessary to exercise to exhaustion. It's best to start out with five to ten minutes of exercise and build up gradually. You don't have to buy expensive exercise equipment or join a gym to get exercise.

An exercise plan should include both aerobic and weight-bearing workouts. Aerobic exercise includes brisk walking, swimming, bicycling (either a regular bike or a stationary one), and using a treadmill or similar equipment. Aerobic exercise strengthens the heart and lungs and may help the immune system to work better.

Exercise is beneficial for everyone and it is particularly helpful for patients recovering from cancer treatments. It can reduce stress, improve energy and alertness, and strengthen muscles.

Weight-bearing exercise builds bone and muscle. This helps people who have lost strength and muscle mass because of cancer treatments or having been on prescribed bed rest. Weight-bearing exercise can be as simple as lifting a few barbells or weights at home or as elaborate as going to a gym and working out with a trainer on sophisticated weight machines.

MANAGING PAIN

People who have metastatic melanoma may have pain because of radiation, surgery, or a tumor. Melanoma may have traveled to the lungs or the abdomen. Radiation or surgery may not cure melanoma at this point, but it can make people more comfortable and may prolong life. Pain from cancer or surgery can almost always be reduced, sometimes dramatically. Pain medications come in many forms: pills, liquids, injections, suppositories, and skin patches.

Some medications are quick-acting and last several hours. Other medications come in a time-release formula. These may take longer to start working, but they also last much longer. Patients may need both forms of medication for the best control of their pain.

Often people are interested in trying non-pharmaceutical methods, such as acupressure, massage therapy, and aromatherapy, to help relieve pain and discomfort. Learning relaxation techniques, meditation, and guided imagery also can help. Guided imagery is the process of using thoughts to focus and guide the imagination. It's based on the concept that the body and mind are connected. Using all the senses, the body responds as though what is imagined is real. For example, people with cancer can visualize their bodies successfully killing off cancer cells. A study published in 2010 in the *Journal of Patient Safety* showed that such activities can reduce pain by more than 50 percent.

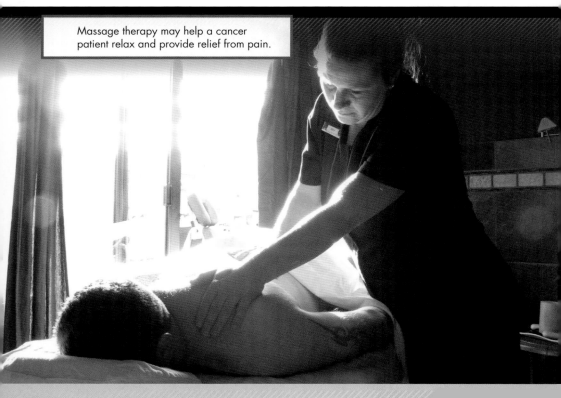

Massage therapy may help a cancer patient relax and provide relief from pain.

GETTING SUPPORT

People recovering from melanoma are likely to experience a wide range of emotions. Cancer patients commonly experience anxiety, depression, insomnia, fear, worry, and feelings of isolation. A doctor or a mental health professional, such as a psychologist or social worker, can be very helpful. This is also the time to turn to family and friends for help and support.

Organizations such as the American Cancer Society, the American Melanoma Foundation, and others listed at the end of this book (see Resources and Websites) can help. These organizations offer online support groups and numerous resources. Such sites can also put people in touch with support groups that meet in their own communities. Patients can learn a lot from one another about how to manage their condition and the physical and mental problems that come with it. Some groups are open to family members and close friends.

Millions of people have recovered from skin cancer. Most of those people only need to have routine follow-up exams by their doctors and to protect their skin from future harm. Some people with advanced melanoma may need ongoing treatment. Survival for people with advanced melanoma is constantly improving.

MaryAnn is currently cancer free. She and her girlfriends sometimes wear T-shirts that say: "Pale. The new tan." MaryAnn sees her doctor every few months to be checked for anything suspicious. She has this advice for people: "Stay away from tanning beds, cover up in the sun, and wear sunscreen. I put it on every single day after I get out of the shower and reapply it later in the day." MaryAnn speaks to the public about skin cancer prevention for the Utah Cancer Action Network. She also volunteers at the Huntsman Cancer Institute in Salt Lake City, Utah.

www.usatoday.com
USA TODAY
Sports
SECTION C

July 27, 2009

From the Pages of USA TODAY

Yanks 'open their hearts'
Kids with sunlight disorder have night to remember

As part of their HOPE Week celebration, the New York Yankees hosted a group from Camp Sundown and the XP Society at Yankee Stadium. What made these children of the dark special is they could visit only at night.

The campers suffer from xeroderma pigmentosum (XP), a rare genetic disease that requires them to stay out of the sunlight. Unable to repair cells damaged by UV light, XP sufferers get blisters, third-degree burns and premature aging of their skin, lips, eyes and mouth. There is no cure and many of them die young from squamous cell carcinoma or melanoma.

Kids who have XP live upside-down lives. Night is day and day is night. They go to school, play sports and attend Cub Scout or Girl Scout meetings at night rather than in the day. When they venture into sunlight, they must be swathed from head to toe in UV-protected clothes,

Xeroderma pigmentosum (XP) is a rare disease that requires people with the disease to avoid the sun. The New York Yankees hosted campers from Camp Sundown for kids with XP at a night game at Yankee Stadium.

Yankees, including pitcher Mariano Rivera *(far left)*, greeted the campers after the game.

sunscreen and sunglasses.

An estimated 250 people in the USA suffer from XP. A large group of them were at Yankee Stadium. First, they took in the Yankees' victory against the Oakland A's from a luxury box in right field. They ate, drank, cheered and received goody bags filled with souvenirs.

Then Yankees players such as catcher Jorge Posada and pitcher A.J. Burnett welcomed them on the field for a postgame carnival that lasted until 3:30 a.m. The kids played Wiffle Ball with Yankees players, and mingled with clowns and musicians.

Katie Mahar, a 17-year-old suffering from XP, says she grew up playing baseball at night with her brothers. She was thankful to the Yankees. "For them to open their hearts and say, 'We want to meet you. We want to spend time with you.' We were like, 'Wow, that's so cool.'"

Katie's parents, Caren and Dan Mahar, founded Camp Sundown as a retreat for sunlight-sensitive kids in 1996. The 60-acre [24 hectares] camp in Craryville, N.Y., has all the usual activities. The kids swim, catch butterflies, go horseback riding. They just do them at night.

Kevin Swinney, a 35-year-old from Spruce Pine, Ala., is a survivor. Diagnosed at 8 months old, Swinney has had countless procedures during his life to remove melanomas and other skin conditions. Kinney's been a regular at Camp Sundown since 2001. He says he won't let the disease stop him from going to baseball games or living life. "XP's not going to stop me," he said. "XP's not going to beat me. I'm going to beat it."

—*Michael McCarthy*

CHAPTER SEVEN

PROMISING RESEARCH

About one out of five Americans will develop skin cancer. That's a lot of people! It's no surprise that scientists are looking for better ways to find and treat all forms of this cancer. Some of the most promising skin cancer research focuses on cancer vaccines, gene therapy, the biology of cancer, new medications, and drugs that boost the immune system.

FINDING SKIN CANCER SOONER

Groups of researchers are working on better ways to find melanoma. One device is being reviewed by the U.S. Food and Drug Administration. Called the MelaFind, the handheld computer-assisted device is an imaging gun that emits ten different wavelengths of light to take pictures of a suspected melanoma. Unlike human eyes, the device can see about 0.10 inches (2.5 mm) below the skin's surface. Another experimental imaging technique uses a handheld laser microscope. The device looks at how cells in the suspected melanoma change reflected laser light.

Doctors hope better imaging devices will reduce the number of unnecessary biopsies. Biopsies are

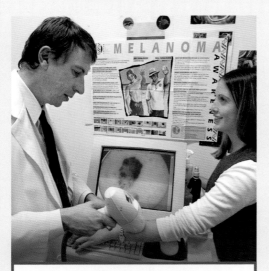

A dermatologist in Australia uses an imaging gun to check a patient's skin for melanomas.

Melanoma? The Nose Knows

You know that dogs have a great sense of smell. Dogs can find children lost in the woods. Dogs can detect traces of explosives or drugs in airport luggage. They can locate people buried under earthquake rubble.

Dogs can be trained to help people with certain medical conditions too. They can smell the dangerously low blood sugar of a person with diabetes. They can smell the chemical changes that come before an epileptic seizure.

Doctors are discovering that dogs can be trained to smell cancer. Cancers produce abnormal chemicals that dogs can smell. In lab tests dogs have correctly identified people with cancer of the bladder, the breast, and the prostate by smelling their urine. They have found lung cancer by smelling the breath. Two studies published in the medical journal *Lancet* showed that dogs could smell the difference between an ordinary mole and a melanoma.

Maybe one day your visit to the skin doctor will include being examined by a lively Labrador or a boisterous beagle!

surgical procedures. They can be painful and may leave scars. For every thirty to fifty skin biopsies performed on a possible melanoma, only one turns out to be melanoma. Patients are sure to welcome ways to reduce unnecessary biopsies.

Other tests focus on tissue taken from a possible melanoma. Instead of a pathologist looking for abnormal cells, scientists can look for certain genetic changes common to melanomas. They search for five particular genes that are present in greater numbers and that are more active in melanomas than in moles. These tests have proven 90 percent effective at telling the difference between unusual moles and melanomas.

CLINICAL TRIALS

Cancer patients may have the chance to try drugs and treatments that are not yet approved for general use. For example, it is especially difficult to treat advanced melanoma. The cancer often does not respond well to treatment. These melanoma patients may have tried all the treatments available to them. They may choose to take part in investigational studies called clinical trials.

A clinical trial is a research study that uses human volunteers to find out how new medications and treatments work. The FDA is the agency responsible for making sure that new treatments are safe and effective. Before the FDA approves a new treatment for widespread use, it must undergo a series of rigorous tests. People who agree to participate in clinical trials sign papers that say they are aware of the potential risks and the possible benefits of trying a new treatment.

Governmental organizations (for example, the National Institutes of Health), medical institutions (such as large hospitals), health foundations (for example, the American Cancer Society), and pharmaceutical companies that develop new medications work together on clinical studies. All new medications and treatments must be approved by the FDA before they can be sold in the United States. The FDA reviews the results of clinical trials to determine if it will approve medications or treatments. Clinical trials consist of four phases. Note that the terms refer to both medications and devices (such as the MelaFind, described earlier in this chapter).

Phase 1   Is the medication safe? Researchers test an experimental drug for the first time in a small group of healthy people (twenty to eighty) to evaluate its safety, determine the right dosage, and identify side effects.

Phase 2   Does the medication work? A larger group of people (one hundred to three hundred) take the experimental drug to see if it is effective against the target disease and to further evaluate its safety.

Phase 3   How does it compare with existing medications? Larger groups of people (one thousand to three thousand) take the drug to confirm its effectiveness, monitor side effects, compare it to commonly used treatments, and to collect information that will allow the experimental drug to be safely used.

Phase 4   Are there other potential uses for this medication, and are there any long-term adverse effects? The new drug or vaccine is approved for sale, but information continues to be collected as more and more people take the medication over a longer period.

MELANOMA VACCINES

Most of us are familiar with vaccines. You have likely received vaccines to prevent measles, mumps, and tetanus, among others. Vaccines trigger the immune system to recognize proteins in bacteria and viruses—proteins that are foreign to the body. Our immune systems produce antibodies (proteins in our bodies that recognize specific bacteria and viruses) to fight infections caused by those organisms. For example, say you cut your finger on a dirty can or step on a nail. The bacteria that cause tetanus may be found on dirty, rusty objects. But most kids get vaccinated against tetanus when they are very young. If a few million bacteria enter your body through the wound, your immune system "remembers" them from when you were vaccinated. The antibodies go right to work to demolish the bacterial attackers.

Cancer cells often evade the immune system because the immune system looks for invaders from outside the body, not for cancer cells inside the body. Usually vaccines are given before a disease strikes in order to prevent it. But scientists are experimenting with giving cancer vaccines to people who already have cancer. The purpose is to teach the body's immune system to recognize cancer cells and to destroy them. Several types of vaccines are being tested for use in patients with metastatic melanoma.

One vaccine is made from a patient's own melanoma cells. The cells are mixed with substances that stimulate the immune system. The patient receives several injections over a few weeks. Although the vaccine has been tested in only fifty-four patients, doctors found it greatly improved survival rates. The tumors shrank in some people and seemed to have disappeared in others. Doctors will follow the patients who participated in the 2009 study for several years to see if their melanomas return or begin to grow again.

Researchers at Harvard University have developed a fingernail-sized implant to carry a melanoma vaccine into the body. The plastic implant is placed under the skin. It releases melanoma antigens (foreign proteins that cause the body to form antibodies) that "reprogram" the immune system to attack melanoma cells. As of late 2009, the vaccine showed remarkable results in mice by destroying their melanoma tumors. The vaccine seems to be more effective than the injectable vaccines being studied in human testing. Clinical trials on humans may start within one or two years.

LOOKING FOR NEW TREATMENTS

Much of the research into skin cancer treatments involves looking for new methods to stimulate the human immune system. The immune system fights cancer in much the same way it fights a bacterial infection. It develops antibodies against the foreign proteins—or antigens—found in the cancer cells and bacteria. The more antibodies an immune system can produce, the better the chance of killing cancer cells. But the immune system may not be able to produce enough antibodies for success.

TRANSGENIC MICE

Enter the transgenic mouse. Using genetic engineering, scientists have developed special mice with human immune systems. These mice can produce completely human antibodies in large quantities. An American drug company is testing a new mouse-generated antibody. Early results showed that 30 to 40 percent of people with advanced melanoma who received this antibody were alive after two years. Sometimes a drug cures cancer. Sometimes it produces a survival benefit. This means that people who took the drug lived significantly longer than people who didn't. The drug is being further tested in clinical trials.

CANCER STEM CELLS

Stem cells from human embryos can grow into bones, brains, lungs, and livers. Scientists also have found adult stem cells in bone marrow and other parts of the body. In 2010 researchers at two Boston hospitals discovered that melanoma has its own kind of stem cells. These cancer stem cells are able to grow and divide despite chemotherapy. This means the cancer can return and spread to other parts of the body. The researchers are looking for a way to stop melanoma stem cells. That would give the body's immune system a better chance at fighting off melanoma.

SEA SQUIRTS

In 2006 scientists working at the Palmer Station in Antarctica discovered that sea creatures commonly called sea squirts produce a chemical that is toxic to melanoma cells. In 2009 researchers announced that they had made a similar chemical in the laboratory. The chemical is named palmerolide for the Palmer Station where the sea creatures were found. More research is needed before the substance can be tested as a medication in people with melanoma. Dr. Dennis Hall, one of the researchers, says, "The potency of palmerolide [in laboratory testing] is exceptional. Melanoma is an aggressive cancer for which there is almost no chemotherapeutic recourse."

TINY NANOTOOLS

The new science of nanotechnology offers a promising way to treat melanoma. A nanometer is one-billionth of a meter. A human hair is about 75,000 nanometers wide. A tiny virus is 50 nanometers wide. Scientists are making tiny nanotools that can enter the body and treat cancer. Researchers have developed hollow golden nanospheres. Each one is about 1/50,000 the width of a human hair. The gold nanospheres are tagged with a protein that directs the nanospheres to the melanoma. The nanospheres are then injected into the patient's body and enter the tumor. Then researchers shine a special type of light on the tumor. The light penetrates the skin and heats up the gold nanospheres. The heat kills the cancer cells but not healthy cells.

MICRO-RNAS

Researchers at the University of Leicester in Great Britain are working to develop a blood test that helps to predict how a person with melanoma will respond to treatment. The test measures a type of molecule called microRNA in the blood of patients with thicker, more dangerous melanomas. Used with traditional staging, this new test can help doctors and patients plan treatment. Patients will have a better idea of their chances of survival even before starting treatment.

NON-MELANOMA SKIN CANCER

Not all research is about melanoma. Researchers are looking at a common plant called *Euphorbia peplus*. They hope to use it to treat precancerous actinic keratoses. It is also proving effective at treating basal cell carcinoma. Scientists have made a gel from the plant's white sap. It seems to cure localized actinic keratoses and basal cell carcinomas more quickly than do current treatments. Basal cell carcinoma seldom metastasizes, but when it does, it is dangerous and difficult to treat. Another experimental medication called GDC-0449 is in phase I clinical trials. It shrinks basal cell tumors with far fewer side effects than other treatments.

Researchers hope to use the plant *Euphorbia peplus* to treat actinic keratoses and basal cell carcinomas.

IT'S IN THE GENES

Science has made remarkable progress in genetic research over the past few years. Researchers have identified and mapped the genetic profile of numerous animals, bacteria, and viruses. They have cracked the genetic code for human beings and identified many of the genetic changes present with some kinds of cancer. For example, people with melanoma often have mutations of certain genes that suppress, or stop, abnormal cell growth. When the genes are damaged, cancer can grow unchecked. This new information about how genes keep us well and make us sick offers exciting new ways to treat cancer.

Investigators have discovered mutations in a group of genes called the PTK genes among some melanoma patients. Mutations in these genes seem to promote the growth of certain types of cancer. Similar mutations have been found in patients with breast cancer. When doctors find these mutations in patients, it tells them that those patients will respond well to certain medications. This means that the same medications—already approved to treat breast cancer—may be effective in treating melanoma as well.

Doctors have long known that people with a large number of moles have an increased risk of melanoma. Now Australian researchers have discovered genetic evidence for the link between the number of moles people have and their risk for melanoma. The researchers counted the moles and examined the genes of six thousand people. They found that mutations in two genes more than doubled the risk of getting melanoma. "This research will be useful in developing screening techniques, and will also allow us to identify potential new drug targets and new therapies to treat melanoma," says Professor Nick Hayward, the leader of the team that made the discovery.

Canadian researchers have discovered a connection between a tumor suppressor gene called the *PTEN* gene and a protein called PKR. PKR normally slows down protein production. When the gene *PTEN* is mutated or damaged, PKR does not work correctly to control protein production. This allows abnormal cancer cells to rapidly multiply and turn into cancer. This link has been found not only in melanoma but also in prostate and brain cancer.

www.usatoday.com

USA TODAY

Life
SECTION D

June 14, 2005

From the Pages of USA TODAY

Genetics may determine who benefits from cancer drugs
Targeted studies show promise

The National Cancer Institute [NCI] plans to change the way it tests drugs in an effort to speed life-saving medicines to patients.

Drawing on a better understanding of the genes and proteins that fuel cancer growth, scientists hope to run smaller, more focused studies of promising new drugs to save time and money, says James Doroshow, the NCI's director of cancer treatment and diagnosis.

Traditionally, doctors have tested cancer drugs on large numbers of patients, with no way to predict who will benefit and who might get worse, says David Johnson, an oncologist and member of the NCI panel that drafted the plan.

As science discovers more of the genes involved in cancer, researchers are custom-designing "targeted" therapies to shut down specific growth signals, Johnson says. That allows doctors to screen cancer patients before beginning a trial, then test drugs only on patients whose tumors have the genetic defect.

"Instead of doing a study of 4,000 to 5,000 people to get an answer, we may be able to do a study of 400 to 500," says Johnson, deputy director of the Vanderbilt Ingram Cancer Center in Nashville.

Smaller trials already have gained approval for a handful of targeted drugs, Johnson says. Under traditional drug testing, studies of the breast cancer drug Herceptin would have required about 25,000 women, Johnson says. Because drug developers knew that Herceptin targeted a defective gene found in about 25% of patients, however, they were able to get Herceptin approved based on research in fewer than 1,000 women.

Running smaller trials could have a downside. Serious side effects may not show up until a drug is prescribed to many more patients, Johnson says. Targeted therapies generally cause fewer problems than conventional chemotherapy, however. And patients with terminal illnesses also might be willing to take greater risks, he says.

Doctors already are performing genetic tests to predict which patients are susceptible to certain side effects, says Grover Bagby, director of the Oregon Health & Science University Cancer Institute. Those tests could make targeted therapy trials even safer, he says.

—Liz Szabo

One day a medication may be developed to correct the mutated gene so that PKR can do its job of slowing down cancer growth.

Researchers at the University of California, San Diego, are injecting melanoma tumor cells with a modified herpes virus. The body recognizes the herpes virus's DNA as foreign. The virus may stimulate the immune system and directly kill cancer cells at the same time. Spanish researchers are using segments of the DNA of a different virus to cause melanoma cells to literally digest themselves. Dozens of other studies involving the genetics of melanoma and other cancers are under way around the world.

Other clinical trials under way that involve skin cancer include:
- Comparing new imaging techniques with other methods of detecting non-melanoma skin cancers
- Trying to prevent the growth of new skin cancers on the face with the chemotherapy drug 5-FU
- Using a drug called dasatinib (normally given to patients with leukemia) to skin cancer patients to see if it reduces metastatic squamous cell carcinoma
- Identifying genetic mutations and other risk factors in melanoma patients and their families
- Combining an experimental melanoma vaccine with a drug called Ontak (used for patients with lymphoma, cancer of the immune system) to see if it improves the body's immune response
- Giving advanced melanoma patients a combination of chemotherapy and a drug called Endostar that prevents new blood vessels from growing around a tumor
- Determining if giving calcitriol, a form of vitamin D used to treat low blood calcium, together with a chemotherapy drug helps the drug to work better against melanoma

Skin cancer is the most common cancer. It's also the most preventable cancer. When found early, skin cancer can often be entirely cured. No one can change their age, their genes, or their gender. But everyone can protect themselves against skin cancer by taking steps such as consistently wearing sunscreen, staying out of tanning salons, and wearing clothing to protect the skin. As a bonus, people who protect themselves from too much sun will have younger-looking skin for more years than those who tan themselves to a leathery brown. Take good care of your skin now and you'll thank yourself later.

GLOSSARY

ABCDE test: a set of guidelines used by the American Academy of Dermatology to determine whether a mole is skin cancer

actinic keratosis: a scaly or crusty growth caused by the sun that may turn into skin cancer

apoptosis: programmed cell death; the deliberate self-destruction of a damaged cell

basal cell carcinoma: the most common and mildest form of skin cancer, which arises from basal cells

benign: a tumor that is not cancerous, does not invade or destroy nearby tissue, and does not spread to other parts of the body

biopsy: the removal of abnormal cells or tissue using a scalpel or needle so they can be studied under a microscope

carcinoma: another word for cancer, as in squamous cell carcinoma

chemotherapy: treatment with strong drugs that kill cancer cells

clinical trials: formal research studies that test how well new medical treatments or medications work in people

cryosurgery: the use of liquid nitrogen to freeze a skin cancer or actinic keratosis. The cancer dies as the skin thaws out.

dermatologist: a doctor who specializes in the diagnosis and treatment of skin problems

dermis: the second layer of skin; it contains connective tissue, blood vessels, oil and sweat glands, nerves, and hair follicles

DNA (deoxyribonucleic acid): the genetic information that determines how our bodies look and work; the genetic information that makes us what we are

dysplastic nevi: a type of mole that looks different from a common mole, that may be larger or have irregular edges, and that may turn into melanoma

epidermis: the outermost layer of skin that contains melanocytes and other specialized cells

immunotherapy: a treatment to boost the immune system's natural ability to fight cancer and infections

interferon: a natural immune system protein used to help the body's immune system. Labs produce larger amounts of interferon to treat cancer.

interleukin: a naturally produced substance that helps the body's immune system;

larger amounts are manufactured in labs to help treat cancer

lymph: the clear fluid that travels through the lymphatic system

lymphatic system: a bodily system composed of vessels, lymph, and lymph nodes; an important part of the immune system.

lymph nodes: masses of lymphatic tissue that are part of the lymphatic system. They collect bacteria, viruses, and cancer cells and help to destroy them.

malignant: cancerous; capable of invading and destroying other parts of the body

melanin: the pigment that gives skin its color and helps protect skin from damage. A suntan is an excess of melanin.

melanocytes: cells in the epidermis layer of the skin that produce melanin

melanoma: skin cancer that begins in melanocytes. It is the most dangerous and aggressive form of skin cancer.

metastasis: the spread of cancer from one part of the body to another, usually through the blood or lymphatic vessels

Mohs surgery: a surgical procedure used to treat cancer in which single layers of cancerous tissue are removed and examined under a microscope one at a time until all the cancer has been removed

mutation: permanent changes in a cell's DNA. These changes can be caused by many factors such as ultraviolet radiation, cigarette smoke, or chemicals. It can be inherited.

nevus: the medical name for a collection of melanocytes; a mole

non-melanoma skin cancer: the general name for skin cancer, such as basal and squamous cell carcinomas, that does not arise from melanocytes

oncologist: a doctor who specializes in the treatment of cancer

ozone layer: part of Earth's atmosphere that helps to protect us by absorbing ultraviolet radiation

photodynamic therapy: a treatment for skin cancer that uses a light-sensitive drug and a special wavelength of light to kill cancer cells

radiation therapy: the use of high-energy radiation from X-rays, gamma rays, neutrons, protons, and other sources to kill cancer cells and shrink tumors. Radiation may be used in the treatment of melanoma.

squamous cell carcinoma: a cancer that comes from the squamous cells

squamous cells: flat oblong cells in the epidermis

staging: the process by which doctors determine if a cancer has spread in the body, helping to plan the best treatment

sun protection factor (SPF): a scale for rating the level of sunburn protection in sunscreen products. The higher the SPF, the more protection it provides against sunburn.

sunscreen: a product that helps to protect the skin from ultraviolet radiation, reflecting, absorbing, and scattering ultraviolet radiation

topical chemotherapy: anticancer drugs in lotions or creams applied to the skin to help cure skin cancer

ultraviolet (UV) radiation: invisible rays that come from the sun and tanning booths. UV rays damage the skin and cause skin cancer.

vaccine: medications used to stimulate the immune system to recognize and help destroy bacteria, viruses, and some cancers

RESOURCES

Actinic Keratoses Net
http://www.skincarephysicians.com/actinickeratosesnet/index.html
847-330-0230

Sponsored by the American Academy of Dermatology, this site provides information about actinic keratoses, precancerous skin lesions, what they look like, how they are treated, and how to prevent them.

American Academy of Dermatology
http://www.aad.org
888-462-DERM

The American Academy of Dermatology is the largest professional association for dermatologists in the United States. It is committed to excellence in patient care, medical and public education, and research. Click on "Public Center" on the home page for a link to information on skin cancer and other skin conditions. Print out the American Academy of Dermatology's body mole map for your own use: http://www.melanomamonday.org/documents/Body_Mole_Map_11-09.pdf.

American Cancer Society
http://www.cancer.org
800-ACS-2345

The American Cancer Society is the leading national voluntary health organization dedicated to eliminating cancer as a major health problem by preventing cancer, saving lives, and diminishing suffering from cancer through research, and education.

Volunteers are available by telephone twenty-four hours per day, seven days a week to answer questions about cancer. The service also answers e-mails from cancer patients and their families. On the website, you can search for information about cancer. Click on "Choose a Cancer Topic" and select skin cancer.

American Melanoma Foundation
http://www.melanomafoundation.org/

The American Melanoma Foundation was founded in southern California by a group of melanoma patients and their families to support melanoma research. The group also promotes community awareness of melanoma. The site has information on melanoma and offers a newsletter.

Centers for Disease Control and Prevention (CDC)
http://www.cdc.gov/cancer/skin/

The CDC's mission is to promote health and quality of life by preventing and controlling disease, injury, and disability among Americans. The CDC conducts research to develop methods to better identify, control, and cure diseases. The skin cancer section of the website includes information about providing shade at school, sun protection and safety, and proper use of sunscreen.

National Cancer Institute
http://www.cancer.gov
800-4-CANCER

This organization is part of the U.S. government's National Institutes of Health. It coordinates the National Cancer Program, which conducts and supports research, training, education, and other programs about the cause, diagnosis, prevention, and treatment of cancer. The site offers free online chats with cancer information specialists.

Skin Cancer Foundation
http://www.skincancer.org
800-SKIN-490

The Skin Cancer Foundation works to educate the public and medical profession about skin cancer, its prevention by means of sun protection, and the need for early detection and treatment. It is the only international organization devoted solely to combating the world's most common cancer. The foundation's mission is to decrease the incidence of the disease through public and professional education, medical training, and research.

Skin Cancer Net
http://www.skincarephysicians.com/skincancernet/index.html

Sponsored by the American Academy of Dermatology, this site provides reliable and extensive information about all kinds of skin cancer and a number of photos of skin cancers. The site shows how to perform a self-examination for skin cancer and has a short video of a doctor examining a person for skin cancer.

WebMD
http://www.webmd.com

WebMD provides detailed health information on hundreds of topics. All content on the website is written and reviewed by healthcare professionals and is updated frequently. Its mission is to provide objective, trustworthy, and timely health information. Search for information on skin cancer in the alphabetical directory or by using the search box.

SOURCE NOTES

8 Caryn Y., interview with author, July 1, 2009.

21 Elizabeth Grice, "Study Finds Unexpected Bacterial Diversity on Human Skin," National Institutes of Health, NIH News, May 28, 2009, http://www .nih.gov/news/health/may2009/nhgri-28.htm (May 19, 2010).

21 Caryn Y.

22 Anne R., interview with author, June 30, 2009.

35 Ibid.

36–37 Alexandria Hudson, "Sunburn Advice Means More to Me Now," *Dallas Morning News*, August 20, 2009, http://www.dallasnews.com/ sharedcontent/dws/dn/opinion/viewpoints/stories/DN-hudson_22edi.State .Edition1.267ae27.html (May 20, 2010).

38–39 Jerry S., interview with author, July 1, 2009.

43 Ginger W., interview with author, December 20, 2009.

50 Caryn Y.

54 Nate Schwegman, quoted in Courtney Perkes, "Skin Scare: I Didn't Think It Would Happen to Me," *Orange County Register*, July 15, 2009, http://www .ocregister.com/articles/schwegman-39694-tanning-melanoma.html (May 20, 2010).

72–73 Ibid.

74 Brian Halvorson, quoted in *Benson County Farmers Press*, "His Presentation Probably Saved the Life of a Student," September 16, 2009, http://www .bensoncountynews.com/archive/2009/091609/news.htm (May 20, 2010).

86 Vincent Cogliano, quoted in Salynn Boyles, "WHO: Tanning Beds Cause Cancer," WebMD, July 28, 2009, http://www.webmd.com/skin-problems -and-treatments/news/20090728/who-tanning-beds-cause-cancer (May 20, 2010).

87 Vincent Cogliano, quoted in USA Today."Tanning Beds Now Listed among Top Cancer Risks," July 28, 2009, http://www.usatoday.com/news/health/ 2009-07-28-tanning-cancer_N.htm (May 19, 2010).

91 Jay Jelinek, quoted in *Benson County Farmers Press*. "His Presentation Probably Saved the Life of a Student," September 16, 2009, http://www .bensoncountynews.com/archive/2009/091609/news.htm(May 20, 2010).

92 MaryAnn Gerber, quoted in Lara Broves, "Tanning Beds Worse Than Sun," *Deseret News*, July 7, 2009, http://www.deseretnews.com/article/705315498/Tanning-beds-worse-than-sun.html (May 20, 2010).

101 MaryAnn Gerber, "Survivor Story: MaryAnn Gerber," Skin Cancer in Utah, EPA website, May 2009, http://www.epa.gov/sunwise/doc/ut_facts_web.pdf (May 20, 2010).

110 Dennis Hall, quoted in Michael Brown and Wanda Vivequin, "Melanoma Treatment Options One Step Closer," University of Alberta ExpressNews, February 19, 2010, http://www.archives.expressnews.ualberta.ca/article/2009/11/10565.html (May 20, 2010).

112 Nick Howard, quoted in "Genes That Cause Melanoma Discovered," ScientistLive, July 6, 2009, http://www.scientistlive.com/European-Science-News/Genetics/Genes_hat_cause_melanoma_discovered/22873/ (May 20, 2010).

SELECTED BIBLIOGRAPHY

American Academy of Dermatology. "Body Mole Map." AAD. N.d. http://www.aad.org/public/documents/Body_Mole_Map_11-09.pdf (February 25, 2010).

——. "Position Statement on Vitamin D." AAD. November 14, 2009. http://www.aad.org/Forms/Policies/Uploads/PS/PS-Vitamin%20D%2011-16-09.pdf (February 25, 2010).

American Cancer Society. "Cancer Facts & Figures." ACS. 2009. http://www.cancer.org/docroot/stt/stt_0.asp?from=fast (February 25, 2010).

——. "Detailed Guide: Skin Cancer—Basal and Squamous Cells." ACS. 2010. http://www.cancer.org/docroot/CRI/CRI_2_3x.asp?dt=51 (February 25, 2010).

——. "Detailed Guide: Skin Cancer—Melanoma." ACS. 2010. http://www.cancer.org/docroot/CRI/CRI_2_3x.asp?dt=39 (February 25, 2010).

——. "Skin Cancer Prevention and Early Detection." ACS. May 21, 2009. http://www.cancer.org/docroot/PED/content/ped_7_1_Skin_Cancer_Detection_What_You_Can_Do.asp (February 25, 2010).

American Melanoma Foundation. "Facts about Sunscreen." AMF. 2006. http://www.melanomafoundation.org/prevention/facts.htm (February 25, 2010).

Ghissassi, F. E., R. Baan, K. Straif, et al. "A Review of Human Carcinogens—Part D: Radiation." *Lancet Oncology*, 10, no. 8. 751–752.

Jablonski, Nina G. *Skin: A Natural History*. Berkeley: University of California Press, 2006.

National Cancer Institute. "Biological Therapies for Cancer." NCI. June 13, 2006. http://www.cancer.gov/cancertopics/factsheet/Therapy/biological (February 25, 2010).

——. "Understanding Cancer Series: Cancer." NCI. September 1, 2006. http://www.cancer.gov/cancertopics/understandingcancer/cancer (February 25, 2010).

——. "What You Need to Know About Melanoma." NCI. March 31, 2003. http://www.cancer.gov/cancertopics/wyntk/melanoma (February 25, 2010).

——."What You Need to Know About Skin Cancer." NCI. July 30, 2009. http://www.cancer.gov/cancertopics/wyntk/skin (February 25, 2010).

National Council on Skin Cancer Prevention. "Position Statement on Vitamin D." NCSP. July 14, 2009. http://www.skincancerprevention.org/News/NCSCPPositionStatementonVitaminDJuly2009/tabid/125/Default.aspx (February 25, 2010).

Sakson, Sharon. "Sniffer Dogs in the Melanoma Clinic." ExaminerCom. April 3, 2009. http://www.examiner.com/x-3791-Pet-Life-Examiner~y2009m4d3-Sniffer-dogs-in-the-melanoma-clinic (February 25, 2010).

U.S. Environmental Protection Agency. "UV Index Scale." SunWise Program. December 3, 2009. http://www.epa.gov/sunwise/uviscale.html (February. 25, 2010).

FURTHER READING AND WEBSITES

BOOKS

Barrow, Mary Mills, and John F. Barrow. *Skin Protection for Life: Your Guide to a Lifetime of Healthy and Beautiful Skin*. Oakland: New Harbinger Publications, 2005. This is an adult book about how to take care of your skin and avoid skin cancer.

Juettner, Bonnie. *Skin Cancer*. Farmington Hills, MI: Lucent Books, 2008. Juettner's book about skin cancer is for readers ages nine to twelve.

Rajpar, Sajjad, and Jerry Marsden. *ABC of Skin Cancer*. Malden, MA: Blackwell Publishing, 2008. This book for adults is about skin cancer.

Silverstein, Alvin, Virginia Silverstein, and Laura Silverstein Nunn. *Cancer: Conquering a Deadly Disease*. Minneapolis: Twenty-First Century Books, 2006. The causes, symptoms, and treatments of cancer are discussed in this book for young adults.

So, Po-Lin. *Skin Cancer*. New York: Chelsea House, 2008. This is another book about skin cancer for teens and college students.

White, Danielle. *Only Skin Deep? An Essential Guide to Effective Skin Cancer Programs and Resources*. Bloomington, IN: iUniverse, 2007. This E-book is about skin care and cancer prevention.

WEBSITES

Clinical Trials
http://www.clinicaltrials.gov

Maintained by the National Institutes of Health, this site is a registry of clinical trials conducted in the United States and around the world. It provides information about each trial's purpose, who may participate, locations, and phone numbers. More than eighty-five thousand trials are listed. You can search for studies about skin cancer.

Intersun Project
http://www.who.int/uv/intersunprogramme/en/

The World Health Organization and other international health organizations have joined together to provide information, advice, and scientific predictions on the health impact and environmental effects of UV exposure; to encourage countries to take action to reduce UV-induced health risks; and to provide guidance to national authorities and other agencies about effective sun awareness programs. A primary goal is to protect children around the world from the harmful effects of ultraviolet exposure.

Melanoma.com
http://www.melanoma.com

This site answers questions about how melanoma is diagnosed and treated. It talks about the risk of melanoma and how to avoid it. Learn how to protect yourself and your family from melanoma. Take the test, "Are You at Risk?" to discover your risk for melanoma. The site is sponsored by a large pharmaceutical company.

Melanoma Hope Network
http://www.melanomahopenetwork.org

This site is dedicated to helping people and families who have been affected by melanoma and has extensive information about melanoma detection and treatment. It includes numerous articles about melanoma and lists clinical trials related to melanoma.

National Coalition for Cancer Survivorship
http://www.canceradvocacy.org/toolbox/11-living-beyond-cancer/

This organization is the oldest survivor-led cancer advocacy organization in the country. Among its many resources is a two-hour audio presentation titled, "Living Beyond Cancer."

National Oceanic and Atmospheric Administration (NOAA)
http://www.srrb.noaa.gov/highlights/sunrise/sunrise.html

NOAA's Solar Calculator allows you to find the ultraviolet index by date, city, longitude, latitude, and time of day. The site includes several countries, so that people who are planning a trip can know the UV index of their destination.

SunWise Program
http://www.epa.gov/sunwise/index.html

Sponsored by the U.S. Environmental Protection Agency, the SunWise School Program is an environmental and health education program that aims to teach children, parents, and teachers how to protect themselves from overexposure to the sun. The program seeks to develop sustained sun-safe behaviors in children. The site also shows a U.S. map with a daily forecast of the UV index to help you know how long you can safely stay in the sun.

TeensHealth
http://kidshealth.org/teen/your_body/skin_stuff/melanoma.html#

This site is sponsored by the prestigious Nemours Foundation, one of the nation's leading pediatric health-care systems. The site has special sections for teens, kids, and parents. You can find information about interesting topics from skin care to skin cancer, school, drugs, fitness, and sexual health.

INDEX

ABOUT THE AUTHOR

Connie Goldsmith is a registered nurse with a bachelor of science degree in nursing and a master of public administration degree in health care. She is the author of *Influenza, Hepatitis, Invisible Invaders: Dangerous Infectious Diseases, Meningitis, Cutting-Edge Medicine, Superbugs Strike Back: When Antibiotics Fail, Lost in Death Valley,* and *Battling Malaria: on the Front Lines against a Global Killer.* She has also published more than two hundred magazine articles, mostly on health topics for adults and children. She lives near Sacramento, California.

PHOTO ACKNOWLEDGMENTS